PLAYS BY
ALAN BOWNE

BROADWAY PLAY PUBLISHING INC
56 E 81st St., NY NY 10028-0202
212 772-8334 fax: 212 772-8358
http://www.BroadwayPlayPubl.com

First printing: December 1997
Second printing: May 2002

ISBN: 0-88145-142-8

Book design: Marie Donovan
Word processing: Microsoft Word for Windows
Typographic controls: Xerox Ventura Publisher 2.0 P E
Typeface: Palatino
Copy editing: Liam Brosnahan
Printed on recycled acid-free paper and bound in the U S A

CONTENTS

An interview from Interview .... *v*
BEIRUT 1
FORTY-DEUCE 35
SHARON AND BILLY 91

From *Interview*, August 1987, by Kevin Sessums

There's a creature known in the South as a feist dog. Little. Scraggly. High-strung. You know where one lives by a backyard full of barks. The thing'll take on a German shepherd—shit, the whole German army— if it thinks its territory is being threatened. But it likes kids too. And it likes the feel of a hand on its underbelly.

Playwright and screenwriter Alan Bowne, whose work concerns the straggly underbelly of life itself, has the friendly tenacity of one of those tight-tailed mutts. "People don't like what I write: Screw 'em," he insists a bone of contention clenched fiercely between his teeth. "That just means they don't like my truth. I don't write Long Island theater. I don't write for the old guard who've been brain damaged on the plays of Eugene O'Neill. I write comedies full of colorful people and I bounce 'em off a black wall."

It's easy to understand, however, how some might wish to avert their eyes from the track marks of humor in Bowne's work. FORTY DEUCE, his first play and later a Paul Morrissey film, concerns a group of male hustlers in a room off Times Square who try to sell a fourteen-year-old to a rich businessman—all the while concealing the fact that the youngster, who lies naked on the soiled bed throughout the play, is dead from an overdose of drugs. Another play, SHARON AND BILLY, is about a brother and sister's guerrilla warfare against their parents in 1950s blue-collar Los Angeles. His next, A SNAKE IN THE VEIN, is scheduled for this fall at Manhattan Class Company and concerns a sage old heroin addict and his young recruit. Bowne's second Morrissey film, *Mixed Blood*, was about a decadent den mother and her young troop of dope-peddling thieves in New York's Alphabet City, sort of a female Oliver Twisted. Yet another Morrissey movie, *Throwback*, is currently in production. Starring Sasha Mitchell, a former Calvin Klein jeans model, it takes us on a tour of the new yuppie mafia and the boxing world in the Red Hook section of Brooklyn. But it is Bowne's latest play, BEIRUT, that is the most controversial of his career. Set in the near future, its subject matter is a plague much like AIDS that has caused quarantining and tattooing of its victims. The two heterosexual characters are barely clothed throughout its 59-minute running time, and the pus of sexuality, enticing as well as toxic, oozes from the work's exposed pores. BEIRUT has caused critics to rail. Clive Barnes bellowed against it, *The Village Voice* labeled it "dangerous."

"*The Village Voice*? What's that?" Bowne bellows back. "It's the left-wing *National Enquirer*. I don't read it. And, to tell you the truth, I don't care what a lisping, rheumy old fart who not only passes out in the middle of plays but also works for a piece of toilet tissue like the *New York Post* thinks about my work."

Bowne didn't start writing until he was 35. Before that? "I bummed around. Drug dealer. Movie extra. Junkie. I worked for a ghost-writing agency. That's why I love New York—there are all kinds of ways to make money. Whenever I run out of money, I come back here. Once I wrote this book about Old Testament women, which I plagiarized out of the New York Public Library. Wrote it for a rabbi in New Jersey who wanted a book for his congregation but didn't speak a word of English. I did business-luncheon speeches. I wrote letters-to-the-editor for sex magazines. I'd be, like, a housewife who had sex with her husband, who has a bad back. I'd throw in a little soft porn. That was the mid '70's and I was getting about 75 bucks a shot for that. I was just never able to do the old nine to five."

Back in New York for a while, Bowne resides in a room on the third floor of a building on 44th street between Ninth and Tenth Avenues. The room has a hand printed plaque—THE HOTEL PIERRE—attached to the door, which Bowne swings open like Loretta Young after a long, long night at the Hollywood Canteen. Inside the room, an old black-and-white television takes up one wall. A bookshelf is crammed into a corner. On one of the shelves *Reagan*, by Lou Cannon, lies atop a spread-eagled book about the greatness of El Greco's art. A used blue towel has been tossed around a bluer electric typewriter, revealing only a cleavage of keys. Also on the desk, a bottle of Sambuca. Bowne pours a bit into an Acropolis-illustrated paper coffee cup. The cloying aroma from the clear liquor fills the room.

"Want some?" he asks.

I nod a no.

"You don't drink? How're you going to make it through the '80s? We had drugs in the '60s and '70s. Got to use whatever you can come up with these days."

Two fans whir away at the summer's humidity. The sounds and smells of 44th—a siren, forgotten garbage, the lilt of Spanish from a mother's mouth—waft in through the open window and become part of the warm, concocted breeze. I place my tape recorder on the pink floral sheets rumpled on Bowne's bed and wait for our conversation to take on the directness of the infamous dialogue of his plays. Sure enough, between sips of Sambuca-ed coffee, he begins to growl away at a number of subjects.

AIDS:

"Nobody owns this disease. There are these AIDS Industry Queens who've taken me on for BEIRUT. If you challenge their preconceptions, then you're in big trouble. And I've always been a troublemaker. Sure, a lot of what I do is dangerous. But that's me. I can't change. I hate being attacked for my subject matter, though. It makes me feel confined, like I'm in some sort of Soviet situation. A lot of these liberals who've attacked BEIRUT are like the Commissars of Virtue. If you don't have the same ideas about virtue that they have—if your ideas are a little more complicated—then they come after you with knives. What they seem to be worried about is that all those people out there are going to be upset because AIDS is going to spread into the straight world. And it seems to me that anyone with at least ten brain cells isn't really worried about that. That's not the really shocking thing about this disease. The scary thing about AIDS is that it happened at all. I mean, this virus that's been here since day one has suddenly decided to mutate and become lethal. We could have a very viral future. And that's what I was dealing with—the sense of the next one up. If AIDS is the first heat in the viral sweepstakes, then the next one might be transmissible by more than two fluids. It's very scary for the future, and nobody can tell me that I can't be scared and deal with my fears as an artist in this regard. I mean—*me*—I'm at risk for this disease. I've boffed guys. I've boffed girls. And I've put needles in my arms. I've covered the waterfront for this disease."

LOS ANGELES:
"I hate it. I grew up in a suburb of the place. Not very good memories. I remember during the Watts riots, my dad hung a big motherfucking American flag on the front porch and sat out there with a rifle in his lap waiting for the black hordes to come up into our yard. He was prepared to blow 'em away. Luckily nobody showed up. Even scared the neighbors away. No, the only way I see living in L.A. now is if I'm writing a screenplay. Then I could live in style. It'd be like living in New York on the Upper East."

ACTORS' EQUITY ASSOCIATION:
"We were doing SNAKE IN THE VEIN at the Limbo Lounge before those Stalinists at Equity shut us down. They drew up all these official-looking papers and said they were going to close us if we didn't contribute to some sort of slush fund with an official-sounding name. We'd already paid the actors. What else do they want? Actors' Equity is run by a bunch of losers who go after people who are powerless. Like playwrights. Then they cave in to the ones in real power. I told them to fuck off."

WRITING:
"I do it to expose my demons. Exposure drives the devil nuts. Billie Holiday knew that. And she was on fucking terms with the devil. But that's how you really frighten the son a bitch—you just get him out. That's what I do when I write. That's why a lot of people don't like my work. I don't pull any punches. I don't tell any emotional lies."

LOVE:
"Living without love is death itself. If you've got love in your life—the true thing—then you've got everything. It's finding the truth of it that's the bitch."

POLITICS:
"Politics is short; art is long. That's my motto. You can get into all this political stuff, but in five years nobody's going to remember. I mean,

you can't write from there, from some political need. If my play started coming true and they were quarantining people and carting them off to camps, then I'd be political in the sense that somehow I'd get out of it. I've always looked at life as an individual. I'm different from most of the people I know in that I'm anarchistic. Any authority really bothers me. Even the authority of those opposed to authority bothers me. Know what I'm saying? I don't deny being selfish. I want as much out of my own life as I can get, under whatever conditions are presented to me. I want to drain the cup."

BEIRUT

For
Michael D'Apice
Brooklyn Boy

BEIRUT originally was workshopped at the Bay Area Playwrights Festival, Mill Valley, CA, in August 1986. Alma Becker directed the production.

BEIRUT received its first Off-Off Broadway production by the Manhattan Class Company at the Nat Horne Theatre in New York City on 23 March 1987, with the following cast and creative contributors:

TORCH . . . . Michael David Morrison
BLUE . . . . Marisa Tomei
GUARD . . . . Terry Rabine

Director . . . . Jimmy Bohr
Set design . . . . Elizabeth Doyle
Lighting . . . . John Hastings
Stage manager . . . . Georgette Lewis

The Off-Broadway premiere of BEIRUT, produced by Barbara Darwal, Peter von Mayrhauser, Maggie Lear, Janet Robinson, and Harold Thau, was presented at the Westside Arts Theater in New York City. It opened 9 June 1987, with the following cast and creative contributors:

TORCH . . . . Michael David Morrison
BLUE . . . . Laura San Giacomo
GUARD . . . . Terry Rabine

Director . . . . Jimmy Bohr
Set design . . . . Elizabeth Doyle
Lighting . . . . John Hastings
Costumes . . . . Walker Hicklin
Stage manager . . . . Laura Kravets

CHARACTERS & SETTING

TORCH, *a good-looking streety male in his early twenties*
BLUE, *a bright, pretty, sensuous female in her early twenties*
GUARD, *with flashlight*

TIME

The near future. Night.

SETTING

A bare, shabby, one-room basement apartment in an abandoned building on the Lower East Side of Manhattan. A crumby sofabed, thin mattress with dirty sheets and pillows. A clock radio. Papers, medical journals, canned goods, and various trash on floor. A sink. Stairs leading down from elevated entrance door. One window with tattered shade.

NOTE: *The style of orthography employed throughout is intentional. So are the bad grammar and odd punctuation. The idiom employed is New York City street. Periods within lines do not indicate full stops but serve, rather, as rhythmic breathing notes. Absence of punctuation indicates that the line should be read in one breath.*

(Darkness)

(Lights dimly up on a human form wadded among the dirty sheets on the mattress)

(Clock radio snaps on; lighting up.)

RADIO D J: *(Voiceover)* ...and this is so old it has hair on it! It's for Skull and his pals out in Flatbush. This one's for you, Skull!

(The refrain of the song, "We Are the World", blasts forth.)

(A man's hand rises from the wadded sheets and slams down onto the radio, cutting it off.)

(Groggily, TORCH sits up edge of bed, covering his nakedness with a sheet. He lights a candle next to bed.)

(Lights up)

(TORCH, in sheet, crosses to sink. Drops sheet, revealing a large "P" tattooed on his left buttock. Throws water on his face.)

(Turning from sink, he rummages in trash for undershorts and slips them on. Squatting, he searches for a can in debris. Can opener. Punches hole in concentrated milk can, drinks. Removes lid from can of tuna and eats hungrily, licking fingers.)

(A siren sounds. TORCH leaps to window, lifts shade, looks out. A flashing light beam stabs him in eyes. Turning from window, he retrieves sheet and huddles on mattress. Hears something. Springs to feet. Stealthily crosses to stairs.)

TORCH: *(In a loud whisper, directed up stairs at entrance door)* Blue? That ain't you, is it?

(No response)

(Despairingly, he crosses back to mattress. Plops down. Flicks on radio, twiddling dial: Strauss's "Zarathustra".)

(As the music plays:)

(The young man begins to caress his body, staring up at the ceiling. Gradually his hands work down to his privates, which he fondles in his shorts. Rolls onto stomach. Slowly begins humping mattress. Suddenly: quick rapping at entrance door. TORCH sits up at once, snapping off radio.)

TORCH: Blue?

(Repeat rapping. TORCH, excited, apprehensive, springs across room and up the stairs to the entrance door. Yanks open door, admits BLUE. They stare for an instant. She is wearing a drab, shapeless dress over soiled sneakers and is carrying a

large purse. Delightedly, she dashes down steps as TORCH, *after a quick look at landing, closes door and turns to look dazedly at girl.)*

BLUE: So lock it.

TORCH: You can't lock it.

BLUE: When's the next patrol?

TORCH: Three A M.

BLUE: OK, we got a few hours.

TORCH: Suckhead! Comin' here. *(Goes down stairs, crosses to window, peers out.)* The whole Lower East's a quarantine zone for doofases who test positive. And you, a negative, send me this fuckfanny underground message that says, "I'm comin' in." Get it through your head, Blue. I'm in quarantine. That's K-U—

BLUE: *(Cutting him off, dropping purse on floor.)* Don't I get a kiss?

TORCH: Fuckin' you know I can't kiss you.

BLUE: *(Approaching him.)* A hug at least?

(He looks into her eyes for a beat. Then grasps her head in his hands, fearful of too much contact, but passionately, touching her forehead to his chest. Abruptly pushes her away.)

TORCH: O K. So there it is. *(Plops onto mattress, wrapping himself in sheet)* That was worth risking your life, or what?

BLUE: It was worth it.

TORCH: How'd you the fuck get in here?

BLUE: F D R Drive. Overpass at East Sixth.

TORCH: When?

BLUE: Early this morning. I holed up in that abandoned building across the street until dark. All day I kept peeking out to see if you'd come to the window.

TORCH: What'd you do, bribe somebody to find me? That's dangerous!

BLUE: Bribes? Your muthah takes bribes. *(Looking around)* You know, I think I liked it better in that bomb site across the street. They put you in *here*?

TORCH: They're runnin' outa places. Least I'm alone here.

BLUE: How long they gonna keep you?

TORCH: 'Till get... lesions.

BLUE: And then what?

TORCH: Then I dunno. Once you got symptoms, they put you someplace else.

BLUE: You got any?

TORCH: I dunno.

BLUE: Can I look?

TORCH: *No! (Wraps sheet tighter about himself.)* Wasn't so cocksuckin' hot I would be covered wit' clothes. Hate to be naked even. Fraid of what I'll see.

BLUE: Torch, I wanna look.

TORCH: Hey! They got a Lesion Patrol for this. They'll be here at three. I'll send you a medical report, O K?

BLUE: *(Stirring cans on floor with foot)* You eating right?

(No response)

BLUE: Hey! Blood-positive does *not* mean! You'll come down with it.

TORCH: Chances are I will. Tomorrow. Next year. I could be here. A long time.

BLUE: You look good.

(Beat)

TORCH: Sodoyou.

BLUE: *(Indicating dress.)* In this? They got everybody in burlap bags out there. *(Starts picking up trash.)* You can go to prison for being "provocative." Calvin Klein's got a reprise of the moo-moo, are you ready? *(Looks up at ceiling.)* It's weird. No sex detectors. God, I am so sick of those little cameras everywhere. *(Twirls)* It's like you're free!

TORCH: They don't care if positives fuck! If you're good as dead, you can fuck like a Sicilian.

BLUE: Shut up. You're not dead.

TORCH: I get *notes* under my door. Girls, guys. "'P' is for positive, we're both Ps, so what the hell?"

BLUE: You must want to.

*(*TORCH *rises from mattress and, swathed in the sheet, crosses to window. Peeks out.)*

TORCH: They say! That repeated reinfectionals *(Pronounce as written)* by this thing? Could bring it on. And just yesterday, I look out in that shitty lot over there? And there's this P-guy. Fuckin' some P-slut! Onna broken wall. Broad daylight.

BLUE: *(Shrugging)* She was probably a prostitute. Every hooker in New York's in here.

TORCH: And negatives sneak in here and fuck 'em too!

BLUE: Well, they can't fuck out there. Sex is a capital crime!

TORCH: *(Turning from window.)* Good! If they stop people boffin', this'll stop. I can't *believe* these stupids, comin' in here and getting infected. This neighborhood's called Beirut for a good reason!

BLUE: I came to Beirut. Am I a stupid?

(Beat)

TORCH: But you. Ain't gettin'. Infected.

BLUE: What's the difference? If I'm caught in here, they'll shoot me.

TORCH: *(Anxious)* But you can get out again?

BLUE: Sure, same way I got in. *(Sits on haunches on bed.)* There's six guys. Hung from lampposts. On 14th Street.

TORCH: There's what?

BLUE: Six blood-negatives. Who were caught in here. Hung by their necks. As a warning.

TORCH: But that's unsanitary!

BLUE: They mean business.

TORCH: *(Stunned)* Jesus. *(Turns away, quickly turns back)* Good! Crime does not pay! *(Suddenly worried)* You can't stay long, Blue. Give yourself plenny time to get out.

BLUE: I won't get stretched, even if I'm caught. God, it is so shining hot. *(She pulls dress over head. She is in bra and panties.)*

TORCH: *(Staring)* The fuck are you doin?

(BLUE sprawls across bed, on her stomach, hugging pillow, twining legs seductively.)

BLUE: Check it out.

TORCH: *I ast you a question!*

BLUE: Cost me plenty, Torch!

TORCH: Get dressed!

BLUE: I wanna show you! I spent a week's salary on this. For Miss Keypunch? This represents an investment.

TORCH: What does?

BLUE: My black market street deal counterfeit decal.

TORCH: This. Is gobbledegoo.

BLUE: Lower my panties.

TORCH: You tryin' to torture me?

BLUE: O K. So I'll do it. *(She lowers her panties, revealing a large "P" very like Torch's on her left buttock.)* See? "P" for positive.

*(*TORCH, *shocked, drops sheet and slowly approaches bed.)*

TORCH: You fuckin. Stupid—

BLUE: So even if I'm caught? I'll just flash 'em my fanny.

TORCH: Dumb shit! You got it onna *left* cheek! *Boy* P's got it onna left. Girl P's got it onna *right!*

BLUE: Oh. So peel it off. Put it on the other cheek.

TORCH: How could you do this?

BLUE: No problem. It peels off.

TORCH: Then a squad guy could peel it off!

BLUE: Those paranoids? They might get their fingers infected.

TORCH: Don't joke *about* it!

BLUE: So would you please peel it off? In case I'm caught?

(Beat. Reluctantly, hungrily, TORCH *descends to bed. Starts carefully peeling off counterfeit tattoo)*

*(*BLUE *murmurs with pleasure.)*

TORCH: I don't wanna tear it.

BLUE: *(Turned on, but trying to maintain composure)* Does it. Look. Like yours? I never saw one before.

TORCH: When I was waitin' my turn? To get mine? I saw lots of guys get... get labelled, they call it. *(Peels it off; snaps her panties back in place)* It's off. *(Regards decal)* It's pretty good, I think.

BLUE: I should check it against yours.

TORCH: *(Intent on decal)* The official tattoo got a very simple design, only they needled these tiny little squiggles in. Before they laid down the color? So it should pick up the light. For the sex detectors. *(Showing her the decal)* See? They got some shine in this too.

BLUE: *(Crouching beside him, very close, looking at decal)* Oh yeah.

TORCH: This is very excellent.

BLUE: Squiggles.

TORCH: Yeah, like little spermoids, see? It would make a very good graphic. Like for a album cover—?

BLUE: It's very sixties I like it. But, Torch, I better check it against yours. Just to be sure it's a good copy.

TORCH: *(Handing it back to her)* Don't gotta bother. It's good.

BLUE: Better safe than sorry. Stand up and turn around.

(TORCH looks away.)

BLUE: You want I should end up hanging from a lamppost? On 14th Street?

(Reluctantly, he stands, his back to her. Crouching, she pulls down the back of his shorts. Holds decal up to tattoo on his left buttock.)

BLUE: I dunno, Torch, yours is like. More detailed. *(Lightly caresses his buttock)* It's not so. Standard. It's got, I dunno. More character. (She licks the tattoo.)*

(TORCH spins around and grabs her hand; they struggle for decal.)

TORCH: *(Starting to laugh)* You slut! Gimme that!

BLUE: *(Holding decal away from him; giggling)* Right cheek is for girls, left cheek is for boys, right cheek is for girls, left cheek is for—

(He retrieves decal, flips her over, exposes her right buttock, and spanks it on with the broad flat of his hand.)

TORCH: *(As he spanks, laughing)* I'm! Gonna teach you! To! Behave!

BLUE: *(Giggling wildly; mock-fear)* Stop it you're hurting me!

(They wrestle, laughing, across mattress. Suddenly, they quiet and gaze at each other. As their lips start to meet, TORCH pushes her away and springs to his feet.)

TORCH: You're a negative and I'm a positive!

(Beat, as he crouches on floor; back to her; and she slumps in despair onto mattress.)

BLUE: I know that.

TORCH: Just lickin' me on my butt like that. This shit is in all the excretals of the body. In my spit? In my sweat? Which is why even a *Trojan* won't protect you! One little abrasion on your skin? And it gets inside of you. No! Intimate! Contact! It's not just smart, it's the law. I got nothin' to do over here but read up on this and I'm tellin' you. You shoul't'nt even be touchin' me.

(Beat)

BLUE: Remember when we first met?

TORCH: So?

BLUE: Remember?

TORCH: Yeah, I remember! *(Beat)* The Sphinx.

BLUE: The Club Pyramid. And how we joked about it? Should we fuck, maybe we shouldn't, and we'd go out and play around and debate this? Places we might do it? When it was safest to try? Like a coupla kids playing with fire. Laughing. Feeling each other up. And then they started those quarantine blood tests and you tested positive and they shoved you in here and it was. Over. Just like that. Most girls? Would of felt lucky they didn't fuck you. My friends, they said you should feel relieved, you were lucky you didn't fuck him. That Torch was a P. Didn't even have a job. *(Beat)* Torch? I didn't feel lucky. *(Beat)* I just felt. Dead.

TORCH: Blue? You gonna live a natural long life. You gonna die in your sleep, with no pain. Or maybe. In a accident. Quick. Clean. No lesions, Blue, are gonna come onto you. And eat you alive.

BLUE: I dream about you. I lay on my bed and I finger myself right into that sex detector. I leave all the lights on, too. Believe it, some computer is getting a scannerful.

TORCH: *(Snickering)* Yeah.

BLUE: I just dream about you.

TORCH: Jerking off is legal. You should use your V C R.

BLUE: *(Disdainfully)* I tried.

TORCH: They got some good porno on there!

BLUE: You're not in any of 'em!

TORCH: A dick is a dick is a cock is a penis!

BLUE: Yours is special!

TORCH: Fuckin' you only saw it that once!

(Beat)

BLUE: *(With a chuckle)* We came close that time, huh?

TORCH: Did we ever. And right the next *day*! They closed off Central Park.

BLUE: What was they gonna do? Put detectors in all the bushes?

TORCH: *(Laughing, rummaging in cans.)* You want some can grapefruit? It ain't cold but— *(Finds can, opens it)* You know the thing I could never stand? About them pornos? *(Drinks from can)* Was that you knew that everybody on there? All those pretty bodies? Was like already dead. Or sixty-five pounds and cacking. *(East Coast slang for "dying")*

BLUE: *(Stretching out on mattress)* You think, back in the old days? I coulda been a porno star?

(He pauses, staring at her.)

TORCH: Yeah.

BLUE: *(Reaching out for can)* Sure, I'll have some.

(Staring, he hands her the can. She smiles at his fixed gaze and starts to drink.)

(Suddenly, he slaps can out of her hand.)

TORCH: *Don't do that!*

BLUE: *Do what???*

TORCH: Jesus, I almost forgot.

BLUE: What's wrong?

TORCH: I told you! It's in my spit!

(He turns away, crouching on floor.)

(Beat)

BLUE: Torch, I don't care anymore.

TORCH: *(Disdain)* Oh. You don't care.

BLUE: There's no *life* out there!

TORCH: No life. Out *there*. But we got lots of that in here.

BLUE: It's *my* risk!

TORCH: *(Abruptly standing; facing her)* Oh right! And I? Got nothin' to say about it! If I infect you? And *you* die? And I'm left here? A carrier? With insects in my blood like fuckin' bullets I shot into you? Then I would find a way, Blue. To off *myself*. As slow. And as ugly. As the way I offed you.

(Beat, as he turns away again)

BLUE: *(Eagerly)* The first thing is to get you outa here. I got in. We can get out. Out to Jersey!

(He reacts with disdain.)

BLUE: I mean, where it's nice New Jersey.

TORCH: Checkpoints at all the bridges! I got no N-card. They'll make me pull down my pants, take one look at my ass, and shoot it.

BLUE: They got N-cards you can buy. Cost a lot, but—

TORCH: I coul't'nt even take a *shit* out there wit'out some detector flashin' on my ass! At *some* point. In every day of your life? You gotta drop your pants. So save your money.

(Beat)

BLUE: So. This is it. We're stuck here.

TORCH: No. *I'm* stuck here. You can go wherever.

BLUE: *(Lies back, languidly)* Do you dream about me? Torch?

TORCH: The fuck does that matter?

BLUE: We could be this V C R for each other. We could just.
Touch ourselves. And look.

TORCH: No.

BLUE: You can't die from looking!

TORCH: I don't trust myself! I might—

BLUE: Trust *me*! *(She rises and approaches him.)* Don't worry. I'll keep it safe.

(He crosses away, sits at foot of bed. She pursues, crouching before him, caressing his knee.)

TORCH: If only—

BLUE: What?

TORCH: If only you could shoot into *me*. Fill me fulla yourself.

BLUE: *(Fingers lightly straying up his leg)* 'Til I spill out of you?

TORCH: I never said this. To no girl ever. In my whole life. I can't shake you, Blue. I can't even whack off unless I— *(Hesitates, as her fingers stray further)* I think about myself *hurting* you. Makin' you. Cry.

BLUE: That's nice. I like that.

TORCH: But I mean *good* pain, you get me? To just blow all this away—

BLUE: With a scream.

TORCH: Yeah.

(Her hand has wandered into his shorts. He grabs it in hammerlock, turning it over, searching it.)

BLUE: *What are you doing?*

TORCH: Lookin' for breaks in your skin! You can get infected touchin' me there!

(She yanks hand away and leaps to her feet, crossing away from bed.)

BLUE: *Jesus!* *(Beat)* I gotta go. *(She rummages on floor for dress.)*

TORCH: No, don't go. We got time.

BLUE: *(Picking up dress; struggling with it, enraged)* Time for what?

TORCH: To talk. To be wit' you—

BLUE: What's the point?

TORCH: I just wanna look at you!

BLUE: I'll send you a snap.

(He crosses to her, rips away dress and grabs her.)

TORCH: You know what I hate about bitches???

BLUE: *(Struggling against him)* Take your hands off me!

TORCH: They hang out wit' you and go I am totally more than my cooz, so fuck off and relate to my beautiful brainpan and *then—*

BLUE: Lemme go!

TORCH: *(Shaking her)* If you just wanna talk and be heady and responsible? She spits on you and does *birdcalls!* Wit' her *cooz!* In your *face!*

(He deposits her on a pile of pamphlets; then he turns away; squats; eats out of a can.)

(Beat)

BLUE: *(Glumly)* That. Is a projection. Of your own inability. Of communication.

TORCH: *(Stuffing his face)* You come here to torture me. You? Are twat-average.

BLUE: *(Springing to her feet)* I am *not!* Like these other girls you been with.

TORCH: *(Rising to face her)* Bitches? *Are torture chamber jokes of some sicko Godhead!*

BLUE: Sure, those girls you hung out with. But I! Am a cut above this.

TORCH: You are basically! The same bitch.

BLUE: I am very. *Very!* Distinct!

TORCH: Your mothah!

BLUE: From these *sluts* you dicked—

TORCH: Yeah?

BLUE: And are now gonna *die* from!

(Beat)

TORCH: Oh. Thanks.

(He turns away, kicking his way through debris to window. BLUE raises, then drops, her hands, crestfallen.)

(Beat)

BLUE: You want I should cook you something? They got a stove in here?

TORCH: *(Peering out window; flat)* No. They give you cans only.

BLUE: Shoulda let me know. I coulda brung you a hot plate.

TORCH: They ration the electricity. You get one minor appliance and a light bulb. They gimme that clock radio and they are short on light bulbs.

BLUE: Jesus, what a hemmeroid this is.

TORCH: It matters? Like you said, I'm gonna die anyway.

BLUE: *(Trying to make a joke)* You're such a bastard, prob'ly you're only a carrier.

TORCH: Oh great. I can stay here the rest of my life. Waitin' for it to show up on me.

BLUE: They'll discover a cure.

TORCH: No, they won't.

BLUE: Oh! So now you're this scientist!

TORCH: It's like the common cold, Blue. Or some flu bugs. It's a kinna virus that changes, as it goes from body to body. You can't vaccinate its ass, you can't cure its ass.

BLUE: Fucking how would you know???

TORCH: I been readin'! *(Picks up stuff on floor; flings it overhead)* The government been crankin' out so much shit on this, you could paper the Bronx. Gas and electric they don't got much of. But shit? About how you're gonna die? Is *free*! They deliver it. Like junk mail around here. I guess it saves 'em on toilet paper.

BLUE: Torch, they are spending millions of bucks on this, and a breakthrough is emanating. There's no doubt in my mind.

TORCH: Blue, half of this city? Is cacked. Or cacking.

BLUE: *(Picking up stray publication from floor.)* And anyway it's good you keep up. You never used to read. I would say like. Iranian? And you would think it was this sandwich.

TORCH: *(Pointing to publication in her hand.)* There's pictures in that one. Of lesions. In full color.

BLUE: *(Quickly dropping publication.)* So? I've seen 'em. They got 'em on posters all over the subways.

TORCH: You mean, like alongside the movie ads?

BLUE: Movies? Torch, Hollywood is toast. They got no stars left. And the ones that are still around? Are very. Heavily. Into make-up.

TORCH: No movies? Where do people go?

BLUE: All the rock clubs are closed. People got too excited they would sweat like pigs it was a health hazard.

TORCH: Don't matter, you should still go out, Blue. Wit' some negative guy.

BLUE: What for?

TORCH: Yeah, I guess you're right. You can't screw him.

BLUE: I don't wanna screw nobody.

TORCH: You know, this is the thing I don't get.

BLUE: Nobody but you.

TORCH: About this fuckin quarantine.

BLUE: You hear what I said?

TORCH: If they was so *sure*. That this bug I'm carryin? Is the thing. That lesionates you. Then *why*? Won't they let you negatives, who have *none* of this cootie in your blood. Have at it wit' each other?

BLUE: *(Exasperated; turning away and kicking off sneakers)* They ain't sure yet what it is, you know that. It maybe incubates and shows up later.

TORCH: Incubate! This is the key conception! I been readin my ass off on this, Blue, and I'm tellin you. This incubate? Is a *crock*!

BLUE: Every three months they test your blood at the office. Just last week we lost a receptionist. And now my boss? Is *very* worried.

TORCH: Lissen to me! The thing is, if you don't know what it is. If you can't isolate its ass and say for *sure*. In the very most scientific labs, Blue. Wit' all the protocols in place and controls and shit. Then you can't yak about this it incubates. If you can't *see* it, spittin' up lesions under a microscope—?

BLUE: *(Turning back to him)* Then you probably don't have it!

TORCH: In shitty vitro and cultured to a fuckin T? Then *how*! Can you demonstrate! To the scientific community! That it *incubates*? You know what I think?

BLUE: *(Lightly caressing his back)* Tell me.

TORCH: I think this bug I got? Is not the only factoral *(Meaning "factor")* here.

BLUE: *(Same; more intimate)* What do you mean?

TORCH: It's bigger than just one thing. Blue?

BLUE: *(Working his back with fingertips)* Rmmm?

TORCH: What are you doin?

BLUE: *(Withdrawing hands)* Trying to relax you. A little massage. Can't hurt.

TORCH: I told you not to touch me.

BLUE: I'll wash my hands after! *(Begins massaging his shoulders with a professional air)* You say there's more to it than this virus you got. So tell me.

TORCH: Feels good.

BLUE: Come on! I wanna hear this.

TORCH: O K. Virus. They say virus. You know what that is?

BLUE: No.

TORCH: It's like when you don't feel good, you go to some doctor, and he can't figure the fuck from what you got. So instead of saying, I'm this stupid ignorant doctor putz-head? He says. It's a virus!

BLUE: *(With professionally interested tones and hands)* I know, it's a disgrace. But you will be happy to hear, Torch, that nobody is going to doctors anymore. Nobody wants to know shit about what's going on in their bodies.

TORCH: Sure! Cause what can they do?

BLUE: Lay down.

(He stretches out on his back. She begins working his legs.)

BLUE: Jack shit is about all. So unless they are employed by the government on this plague? All the doctors are going out of business.

TORCH: *(Incredulous)* You mean. Like even those manicure doctor snots wit' those. Those fuckin' chicky brownstone offices onna *Upper East*?

BLUE: Closing up shop. Anyway, their rich patients left New York months ago. For the French Riviera or someplace.

TORCH: Oh sure. This lowlife virus would *never* go to the French Riviera.

BLUE: *(Straddling him; professionally working his pecs)* Yeah, I guess they think that.

TORCH: This scarlegged virus would not fit in onna Riviera. Can you just see it? Stretched out onna beach?

BLUE: Tryin' to get a tan?

TORCH: Wit' sunglasses? A big cigar?

BLUE: And a frozen daiquiri! *(They embrace, giggling.)*

(Suddenly, she pulls back; professional again, as she massages him.)

BLUE: So. If they say it's a virus, this means they don't know what the hell it is and they are just fucking with us.

TORCH: Right!

BLUE: *(Massaging his stomach.)* I suspected this.

TORCH: Viruses are the stars. Of the Rowdy Doody Show. Which is so popular all over the medical world today. Now, you got your parvo- and you got your retro-viruses.

BLUE: *(Massaging deeper; impressed)* Yeah?

TORCH: And the retros invert your T-cell ratio.

BLUE: Jesus.

TORCH: They invert and revert and pervert, all up and down your— *(Enjoying massage)* That's nice, Blue. All up and down your cellular organization. Replicating! Like the dancing dead! In some old l980s monster movie.

BLUE: *(Massaging lightly around his basket)* It's frightening.

TORCH: But to go lookin' for *one* virus only, is a stupid. You know what I think?

BLUE: Tell me, I wanna know.

TORCH: I think— *(Squeezing his legs together)* Don't do that.

BLUE: It's your tension spot. I went to massage school, and I know. Some people, all your stress is concentrated here.

TORCH: *In my balls?*

BLUE: *(Crisp and professional; spreading his legs.)* Spread your legs. Just *under* your balls. It's a neurovascular nexus of tension. Stress is bad for you, Torch.

TORCH: *(Relaxing)* Yeah. They say that you shoul't'nt get stressed. Is that funny? They quarantine you onna Lower East Side and say. Don't get nervous.

BLUE: It's very important you stay calm. *(Working his genitals through underwear.)* I'll be real gentle here. Now what's your idea on this virus?

TORCH: It's a. Piggy-back. Virus.

BLUE: *(After a quick, confused beat)* It's what?

TORCH: For this bug I got? To be operational? *(As she straddles him, working his pecs, he reaches up and tentatively fondles her breasts.)* It gotta combine. It gotta sorta— *(Fondling her hungrily)* Get humped. Dog style. By a *parvo*-virus. See?

BLUE: So you gotta have both kinds of virus in your system?

TORCH: Right. Lemme just smell you, Blue.

BLUE: *(As he buries his nose in her breasts.)* So why. Don't they test for this?

TORCH: Lemme taste you.

BLUE: *(As he licks at her breasts.)* You should tell these people. To start. Testing on this.

TORCH: I dream about you, Blue.

(She cradles his head and begins slowly, lovingly, grinding her crotch into his.)

BLUE: *(Undulant, lost in pleasure)* They can grow babies in test tubes now. So why can't they locate. A coupla viruses. Committing sodomy. In your veins?

TORCH: Blue! Don't. Do that.

BLUE: Baby, we got our underwear on.

TORCH: That's pretty thin fabric down there, Blue.

BLUE: I'll pull away in time. We can dry-kiss, too.

TORCH: *(Startled)* Fuck is that?

BLUE: It's a new thing. You just. Rub lips. You don't French or nothin. Try it.

TORCH: I don't wanna.

BLUE: Like this. *(She brushes her lips against his.)*

TORCH: I don't like it.

BLUE: Try it again!

(She grabs his chin and brushes his lips with hers. Then they rub faces all over, slowly, sensuously, as they grind their hips together.)

TORCH: *(Very, very tenderly)* I could. Rip off your tits. Wit' my teeth.

BLUE: *(Also)* I'm gonna. Squeeze your balls. 'Til they pop.

TORCH: I'm gonna. Gang-bang you. All by myself.

BLUE: I'm gonna rape. Your tush.

TORCH: I'm gonna love you. 'Til I die.

(Beat)

(Their open lips begin hungrily to meet.)

(A loud pounding at entrance door)

GUARD: *(Offstage)* Lesion Squad!

(TORCH and BLUE scramble to their feet.)

TORCH: Ace the candle!

(BLUE blows out candle. Darkness.)

TORCH: *(Hissing)* The fuckers come early!

GUARD: *(Offstage)* Respond in kind!

TORCH: Where we gonna hide you?

BLUE: I dunno!

GUARD: *(Offstage)* Hey! Number two dash fifteen dash six! You in there?

TORCH: Jesus!

BLUE: I got my "P" decal! We'll show him that!

GUARD: *(Offstage)* Time for your checkup! Get to the door or we're coming in!

TORCH: *(Calling, off)* Be right there! I was sleepin'! *(To* BLUE, *hissing)* Hide someplace.

*(*BLUE *crouches at side of stage as* TORCH *stumbles in the dark for door. Climbs stairs clumsily.)*

(Door opens as he is halfway up stairs. A flashlight beam freezes him. There is the dim form of a soldier in the doorway, backlighted.)

GUARD: O K, O K. Back off.

(Flashlight beam follows TORCH *back down stairs.)*

GUARD: Drop your shorts.

(Silhouetted, back to audience, TORCH *pulls down his undershorts.)*

(The bright beam plays over front of his body.)

GUARD: Lift your arms, goddamn it.

*(*TORCH *does so. Beam travels from one armpit to another. Stops.)*

GUARD: What's that?

TORCH: A mole. We been through this.

GUARD: O K.

(Beam descends.)

GUARD: Come on! Lift 'em up! We ain't got all night.

(We see TORCH's *arms move, lifting his genitals.)*

GUARD: O K, O K. Come on, you know what to do.

*(*TORCH *turns around. Beam searches his buttocks.)*

GUARD: Fuckin' plaguey. So crack a smile!

*(*TORCH *bends over.)*

GUARD: What a job I got. O K, you're clean.

(As TORCH *pulls up his underwear the beam abruptly scans the room, darting everywhere. A crash, as* BLUE *falls over something, trying to escape the beam.)*

GUARD: Who's that?

TORCH: A hooker!

(Beam shoots to TORCH's *face.)*

TORCH: I got a hooker down here.

GUARD: You having a nice *vacation* in Beirut?

TORCH: See, it's like this. I coul't'nt sleep and—

GUARD: *Get her over here!*

TORCH: *(Into darkness)* Get over here. *(Beat; hissing)* Hey. Bitch!

BLUE: I'm coming! *(Beam shoots to illumine her.)* I tripped and hurt my leg.

TORCH: *You O K?*

(Beam shoots back to him.)

GUARD: What do you care?

BLUE: I'm here. I'm here.

(She crosses, limping, to stand in front of TORCH, their backs to audience, in the glow of the beam.)

GUARD: Never seen you before.

TORCH: She just got Q'd. Today.

GUARD: What's your number?

BLUE: *(Quick)* Three dash six dash sixty!

GUARD: Show me your label.

TORCH: Sure. She got one.

(TORCH turns BLUE around, yanks at her panties, showing the decal, the beam following all this.)

TORCH: See?

GUARD: Very. Very. Nice. Turn around, honey.

(She does so, adjusting panties. Beam plays slowly over her body. Stops.)

GUARD: What's that?

BLUE: Where I bumped myself just now.

GUARD: *(Puts beam in TORCH's face.)* Show me her tits.

TORCH: What?

GUARD: I have to check everybody. Now show me her tits.

BLUE: I'll show you.

GUARD: Him! I want him to do it.

(Their backs to audience, TORCH lowers her bra, the beam following.)

GUARD: Oh man. Rub them.

TORCH: Mister? What is this—?

GUARD: *(Beam shooting back and forth from* TORCH's *face to hers.)* You guys got no symptoms yet. I hardly ever see that. She's not on my list. It's after curfew. Now rub her tits, butthole.

*(*TORCH *hastily begins to do so.)*

(Loud zipping sound)

TORCH: So, Mister. Is this O K?

GUARD: Show me.

TORCH: Show you what?

GUARD: *Show me her bush!*

(Beat. TORCH, *with immense tenderness, begins peeling away her panties.)*

(Heavy breathing sound from GUARD.*)*

(Sound of a siren)

GUARD: Shit! A break-in!

(Muttered curses as GUARD *struggles with zipper, the light making crazy patterns on floor and ceiling.)*

(Siren out, beat)

(Final zipping sound)

(Beam of light shoots to their faces.)

GUARD: I'll see you two. In the morning.

(Beam disappears. Door slams.)

(Darkness)

(Beat)

BLUE: *(Exhaling)* Jesus, Torch.

(Sounds of stumbling in the dark)

*(*TORCH *finds and lights candle.)*

(Lights up)

TORCH: Get dressed. You gotta get outa here.

BLUE: *(Angry)* I'm gonna be sick!

TORCH: Oh! But me? I feel like a David's cookie!

(He rummages on floor for her dress; hands it to her.)

BLUE: Torch? You got a little sympathy here?

TORCH: You ain't gettin dressed!

BLUE: What's *wrong* with you?

TORCH: Wanna stick around? Be a Barbie doll? For *soldiers*?

BLUE: Why the bum's rush? You got a kind word for me maybe?

TORCH: Yeah: Go back to Flushing!

BLUE: *(Casting away dress.)* When I'm good and ready!

(Beat)

TORCH: I get it. You *liked* it.

BLUE: Liked *what*?

TORCH: Watchin me crawl for that United States scumhole of a National Guard masturbator!

BLUE: That's a lie!

TORCH: Sure, this is a *revenge* thing for you.

BLUE: Did it ever cross your brainpan. That we could face this shit *together*?

TORCH: So fuck it, let's just hang my balls! Over the door! So he should know when we're ready!

BLUE: Torch, we'll be *stronger* the next time!

TORCH: Maybe he'll make you go *down* on me. And I could stand there and whistle like. Zippidy-do-dah!

BLUE: I am so sick of you.

TORCH: You! Got your head! Up your cakes!

BLUE: *(Striking him)* You rat bastard!

(He grabs her by wrists, slams her against wall.)

(Beat)

(He slaps his forehead and turns away.)

TORCH: I need some drugs.

(Beat)

BLUE: *(Verge of tears)* If I wanna stick it out here? Then I'll stick it out here!

(He turns, stares at her.)

TORCH: Oh *yeah*? *(Beat)* Let's play a game!

BLUE: *(Same)* You're on.

TORCH: It's kinna scary, Blue.

BLUE: *(Turning sarcastic)* Oh. Hey. A change of pace.

TORCH: I call this game: "The Soldier? And the big. Brave. Uterus."

BLUE: And which. Are you?

TORCH: *(Cold)* Get on your knees, honey.

BLUE: *(Smirking)* I'm gonna win this game. Lootenant.

TORCH: *I gave you a order!*

(Beat)

BLUE: *(Defiant)* O K. I'm woman enough for whatever you wanna play, Torch. *(Sinking to knees)* Are you man enough?

TORCH: Crawl.

(On all fours, she crawls to him. Reaches up to pull at his shorts)

(He whacks away her hand.)

BLUE: *(Stung)* Hey! Nipplehead! That hurt!

TORCH: Naughty naughty. You shoul't'nt make a move I don't tell you. Now beg me to fuck you.

BLUE: Torch. This is me. Your girlfriend. From Queens.

TORCH: You want it? So beg me for it.

BLUE: I am *not*! Quaking with fear here.

TORCH: *(Turning ugly)* I told you to beg!

BLUE: *Come on, Torch—*

TORCH: *(Grabbing her by chin)* Beg me for it!

BLUE: *(Struggling to free herself from his grip)* Get off!

(He has her by throat.)

TORCH: And in every drop of me? Gonna be a trillion tiny cockroaches that gonna float around inside of you and poop out their shit! *Real slow!* Into your body. For like a year? Five years? Maybe longer. And all this time you're worryin about a freckle that wadn't there before. Feelin' in your pits for *lumps*! Havin cold sweats every time you *cough*! Checkin' yourself out every hour of every day till this body you got? This body you think is so hot?

BLUE: *(Gasping)* You're choking me!

TORCH: Starts to look like what it really *is*! A wax paper bag fulla livers and turds that puts coffee stains on your underpants and snot in your water glass! *I hate my body!* *(Thrusts her to floor)* And I hate yours too, bitch. *(He steps over her, crosses to her purse. Crouches, rummages in it)* You bring me any cigarettes?

(BLUE is panting painfully on the floor, grasping her throat.)

(He finds a cigarette pack in the purse; starts to rip it open, stops.)

TORCH: You believe this? They still got that sucky warning onna pack. "The Surgeon General..." Is *dead*! Of the plague. *(Rips out a cigarette, rummages for match)* Fuckin' asshole. Prob'ly thought, *I'm* healthy. I never smoke. I have nice clean sex too. We're very responsible up here. I never muffdive my wife. Mainly? I jog! I eat alfalfa sprouts I avoid salt I— *(Exploding; casting purse away)* Where's a fuckin match???

(Beat)

BLUE: *(Flat)* Use the candle.

TORCH: Oh, right. *(He crosses to candle; lights up from it. Inhaling)* Unfiltered Camels? Are the greatest invention. Of American history. *(Exhaling)* Is what I think.

(TORCH throws himself onto mattress.)

(BLUE manages to rise to her feet. Looking away from him, massaging throat, she crosses to sink; wets lips.)

BLUE: *(Strained)* The Plasmatroids? Got a. New album out.

TORCH: Any good?

BLUE: Coupla cuts.

TORCH: They only play that one cut on the radio.

BLUE: Which one?

TORCH: "Beep. Beep. You're Dead."

BLUE: *(Towelling her face with stray rag)* There's a hotter one. "Pneumocystis Carinii Killed My Dog." Heavily metallic, but with a jazz riff double-tracked.

TORCH: I miss my stereo. I miss my earphones.

(She crosses to purse, crouches, extracts cigarette, easily finds a match, lights up.)

(Beat)

BLUE: *(Eagerly)* Maybe I got it too!

TORCH: Maybe you do. But far as they can tell? From blood tests? You don't. So far you're safe.

BLUE: Safe from *what*?

TORCH: Don't be a asshole.

BLUE: *(Looking around)* Anyway, I like it here. *(Wandering about)* You can do anything you want here. Nobody cares. Nobody's watching.

TORCH: They got some pretty horny guards here, you may have noticed.

BLUE: I know how to handle him!

TORCH: You was scared shitless of him!

BLUE: Don't *worry* about it! I got a plan for that guard. The thing is, I like it here. It's a hole, but we could fix it up. We could requisition some curtains. There's an old armchair in that lot over there—

TORCH: *(Sarcastic)* Hey! Let's set up house and have a baby!

BLUE: So fucking why not???

TORCH: Who at six months of life? Gonna start gettin' these. Purple scabs—

BLUE: It's not a hundred percent infection!

TORCH: Almost!

BLUE: You'd make a shitty father anyway.

TORCH: Blue! I'm a major risk category!

BLUE: *(Flipping cigarette into sink)* You were always a risk! Even before this plague.

TORCH: But *pre*-plague? Nobody never. Ever. Fuckin' *died* from some sucky love thing. You maybe got hurt, but you got over it. Now you put on your dress and you get your ass outa here. You go back and—

BLUE: And what?

TORCH: I dunno! Whatever. You get into somethin!

BLUE: Macrame?

TORCH: This is not my problem.

BLUE: My job! I could get into my job. Last week? We tabulated accounts. For a Filipino dry cleaners. Torch! I never saw the *beauty* in this before—

TORCH: You live, that's all! Whatever that means, you live.

BLUE: You can't *live*! Without love. You just. Can't.

TORCH: Lotsa people! *They* live. Wit'out *once*! Lovin' one shitty flick on this planet—

BLUE: *So?* They are walkin' around dead!

TORCH: Priests, what about them? Never *once* can they flick—

BLUE: Priests love God!

TORCH: So love God!

BLUE: I love *you*! *(Beat; as she kneels on bed)* You can't live without it, Torch.

(TORCH springs from mattress; flips cigarette into sink and strides about room as:)

TORCH: This? Is a canary! Before I met *you*? I ditn't love *nothin'*. And I was O K. I could take it or leave it. I walked around, hadda coupla beers, hung around at O T B, told funny stories to the unemployment, and then. At night? I would go to some club and lissen! To this cunt over here? Or that cunt over there? Drool at me about this *love* intestine! And I would laugh. And then fuck her. Or not fuck her. It ditn't matter. I was happy.

BLUE: You were dead.

TORCH: *(Ignoring her; lifting shade at window.)* Jesus! If I was blood-negative? I would be out there, breathin' so free. Who needs *sex*? I would go. To a ball game. I would flash my N-card so casual and get on that subway take the B M T over the Manhattan Bridge to Brooklyn. The city looks great from that bridge. Or maybe I would go to like Bensonhurst? You're Queens, you don't know. But me, I'm Brooklyn Italian and Bensonhurst? Is great! These old Italian guys? Hangin' out in front of gelati cafes and watchin the girls—

BLUE: In shapeless sacks.

TORCH: Don't matter! *Cugines? (Meaning buddies or regular guys of the Brooklyn streets. Based on Italian, pronounced "koo-sjeens.")* Got X-ray vision! And the goomadas *(Phonetic Italian for grandmothers; accent on second syllable)* and the baby carriages—

BLUE: Babies? Torch, they kill you out there if you get pregnant.

TORCH: *So who needs kids?* Fuckin' brats, they can raise 'em in test tubes now! I heard it onna radio! Big breakthrough. Culture the race in jars or some shit. No exchange of virulous fluids!

BLUE: *So who wants to be born in a petri dish?*

TORCH: So there's baseball and stickball and 86th Street Brooklyn! Everybody on that street, boppin' around, flirtin', eatin' take-out—

BLUE: *Nobody!* Is boppin around out there, Torch. No stickball. No flirtin. No life. Don't you get it? Without love to look for? Without sex at least? There's nothin'.

TORCH: *There's pizza! (Beat)* Now just. Get outa here. You make me. Sick.

BLUE: Right. My body is this bladder sack with turds floatin' around in it. I heard you. Now if you don't get over here. And fuck the stuff outa me? Within the next say twelve minutes? I. Am gonna pee. On your mattress.

(Beat)

TORCH: What if you die from it, Blue? And I gotta live with that?

BLUE: Come over here.

TORCH: Answer me!

BLUE: Come over here and I'll tell you.

TORCH: Tell me from there! I wanna hear this. How I. Can sit here. And watch those nice little tits of yours? Shrivel up like raisins. Sit here and watch you lose like fifty pounds in twenty-four hours. While your *head*! Puffs up! To twice its size! And that I done it to you. This I wanna hear.

(Beat)

BLUE: You want pizza? You got pizza. With this decal I can sneak out and
sneak in. You want stickball? You got it. Wanna get drunk? Wanna nice
t-shirt? It's all yours. And if one of us starts to die? Then a light meal,
a glass of wine, and four grams of seconal. (Beat, as he stares at her.)

BLUE: Two grams apiece. We could go to sleep in each other's arms. Naked.
So the guard should get off on it.

TORCH: *(Staring)* You gonna get serious? Or what?

(BLUE stretches out and smiles.)

BLUE: I *am* serious. You really like my tits? I never thought you did.
My ass maybe, but—

TORCH: I could really see this. Oh sure. You and me playin' house in here.
On Sundays we take a little stroll inna park. You seen Tomkins Square
lately? It's where they pile the bodies. And burn 'em on Sundays. We could
walk around, sniffin' the fresh air. We could watch the people who can't
control themselves? Squattin' in the gutters wit' the shit runnin' outa them
like rusty tap water. Or! We could go to the laundromat on Avenue A? And
watch people tryin' to unglue the t-shirts from their sores to wash 'em. And
then! Come back home and *fuck*! Wit' two water glasses and a killer dose of
reds in this little *altar* next to the bed! *(Nods madly.)* It's the American Dream!

BLUE: I usta think that too.

TORCH: *Think what?*

BLUE: That life was over here, and death was way over there. That they
don't mix. But *now*? They're joined at the hip.

TORCH: What we need here! Is some adult maturity!

BLUE: It's a lovely thing you're feelin' for me. How you don't wanna infect
me and all? But stick it up your ass, *all right?*

TORCH: I ain't lissenin' no more!

BLUE: Because I got two choices. First, I can live without risk and feel dead.
Or second? I can risk death and feel alive. *I would not be the bitch that fell for
a prick like you if I would choose the first!*

TORCH: *I never liked your tits!* Very seldom. Do you find a decent pair of tits.

BLUE: Yeah? Well, *testicles?* Are a turn-off!

TORCH: Either they got cow udders or pimples!

BLUE: And I bet that *you*! Got the kinna testes that flap against a girl's ass
when you fuck her! Whap! Whap! Whap!

TORCH: Tits that are nice and firm and just the right size—?

BLUE: It drives you crazy! Cold wet dog balls beatin' time on your ass—

TORCH: *Suicide!* Is a sin! It's anti-nature. Un-Italian! And non-American!

(He crosses to sink, grips it, not looking at her. During following, she rises from mattress and approaches him; finally, she begins caressing his back.)

BLUE: You had a choice about gettin' this disease? Or you had *one* word to say about *one* thing that has happened to you in your whole life, including you got born? No. It was always other people or god or some shit that made your choices. You ain't owned *one* minute of your life, Torch. But that moment you die? You can choose it. You can choose when, you can choose how. You *own* it, Torch. You don't wanna give me a baby? O K. Then give me that moment. That moment when we die. It will belong to us, Torch, and to nobody else.

(Beat, as he feels her body on his back. He breaks away, crossing to radio.)

TORCH: You wanna lissen to some music? *(Twirls dial)* Popular? Classical? Jazz?

BLUE: All I'm sayin', is it don't have to be a sin!

TORCH: *(Abandoning radio.)* You end up in hell!

BLUE: Oh my god! *(Looking about in mock-terror at sleazy room)* How will we *handle* it?

TORCH: Shut up! *(Grabs sheet, covers himself with it)* And go home. *(Huddles on bed under sheet)*

BLUE: *(Sitting on mattress.)* So. That's settled. I'm gonna get curtains for in here. And as for that guard? I know what to do about *him*. Got the idea from this T V program they showed the other night, N B C, coast to coast, about plagues like in Europe hundreds of years ago? This was supposed to make us. Feel *better*? I dunno. Anyway, they told how the people who got the Black Death? A more Christian disease than what we got now, I mean you died in a matter of mere days. How these people who caught it got very pissed off about the ones who didn't catch it. So the sick ones would sit by their front windows until well persons passed by on the street? And then suddenly reach out! Grab them! And *breathe* into their faces! People. Never. Change. *(Beat; chuckling)* So that's what I'll do to that guard. When he's good and hot, I'll ask him to come closer. And then *breathe* on him!

TORCH: *(Under sheet)* This thing here is not airborne! It's a fluid transmission only!

BLUE: Thank you, doctor. *So I'll spit on him!* We can always scare him off, scare him so bad he'll stop bothering us. There's power in being sick, Torch.

(Beat)

TORCH: Blue?

BLUE: Yeah?

TORCH: I got a hard-on.

(Beat)

BLUE: Me too.

TORCH: But the thing is, you can't have it.

BLUE: Come out from under there. I want you to look. In the candlelight? There's these little specks floatin in the air. Little animals just waiting. To kill off the things that get weak. They float and turn and dance in the light. Come on. Look.

TORCH: *(Still under sheet)* No.

BLUE: O K, so here comes a microbe!

(She gets under sheet with him; we see only their forms under it, rolling about.)

TORCH: Stop it!

BLUE: I'm a germ! I'm gonna kill you!

TORCH: You can't *do* this!

BLUE: Call out the National Guard!

TORCH: You gonna haveta do this, Blue, all by yourself. *(Big, emphatic)* It ain't. My. *Responsibility!*

(Beat, as their forms freeze beneath sheet.)

BLUE: You dickless dink. Of a cop-out.

TORCH: Huh?

(BLUE whips away the sheet and stands up over him, enraged.)

BLUE: I bet you been tellin' that to girls. *Your whole life!*

TORCH: *(Sitting up.)* The fuck is that suppose to mean?

BLUE: Men? Are *pussies!*

TORCH: Who?

BLUE: Always like— *(Sarcastic macho mimicry)* She *begged* me for it! Wadn't *my* fault if she got hurt! The stupid cooz!

(TORCH grabs her and pulls her down onto mattress; rolls her onto her back; into her face:)

TORCH: Hey. Bitch! You wanna get lucky, or what???

BLUE: *(Struggling beneath him)* I can just see you! If I come down with this? You gonna be crawlin' around here goin. It wadn't *me. She* asked for it. I was just this. Innocent bystander!

TORCH: Jesus, I never met such a fuckhead! So we won't do it! So get outa here!

(She flips him over; into his face:)

BLUE: You say it.

TORCH: Say what?

BLUE: That you wanna be *inside* me! *(Beat)* That what you feel, I gotta feel. That what I gotta face, you gotta face.

(Beat)

TORCH: You are some kinna fazool. Some kinna magazine. Like "Modern Romance", like "Teenage Love", like—How'd I ever fall in love wit' you? In the middle! Of a disease???

BLUE: Piss on this love you got! I don't want excuses here, Torch.

TORCH: So what *do* you want?

BLUE: I want you to climb inside me. And never leave.

(Beat)

TORCH: I get it. You want my soul, right?

BLUE: That's right.

TORCH: Typical bitch.

BLUE: That's right.

TORCH: Eight inches of dick ain't enough for you, hey?

BLUE: *(Contemptuously) What* eight inches?

TORCH: Give or take a centimeter!

BLUE: Good-bye. *(She angrily rummages in debris for her dress.)*

TORCH: Fuckin' how can this be? You love somebody and don't wanna give 'em a disease? And that makes you this. *Sonofabitch?*

BLUE: *(Pulling dress over her head)* Pre-plague? You woulda said, Hey you! Wit' the face! You gettin all hung-up and hurt here? So it's your *own* fuckin fault, you chee-chee! *(Slang for cheap girl)*

TORCH: It's not the same!

BLUE: *(Smoothing dress; grabbing up purse; rummaging in it)* It's the same.

TORCH: Bitches in a plague? Are sows in shit!

BLUE: *(Throwing packs of cigarettes at him.)* Here's some extra cigarettes. *(Again rummages in purse.)* And somewhere. In here. I brung you a Mars bar.

TORCH: Under your thumb, that's where you want us. In a fuckin' cage which only you got the key! Well, lemme tell you, wit' a guy? It's different! He wants a good time, a nice fuck, a few laughs, and then. He wants. To go out. *And play some pool!*

(Beat, as she pauses, looking at him.)

BLUE: What. Are you talking about?

TORCH: We'd be trapped here! Lookin' for spots on each other alla time. I can't live inside of you, Blue, in some kinna romantic magazine. Even if I forget and drink outa the same glass as you? Much less fuck you? I would hate myself.

BLUE: Guys always do.

TORCH: Do *what*?

BLUE: Hate themselves after fucking. You guys can have this Fourth of July experience up a woman's vage and still feel like total shit afterwards. Why is that?

TORCH: You keep changin'! The subject!

BLUE: The subject! Is you got no *balls*!

TORCH: Fuckin' *what*? I don't wanna *murder* you! Is that O K?

BLUE: No, I won't eat that.

TORCH: It's the truth!

BLUE: I gotta go.

TORCH: What, I'm some kinna limp! wimp! Cause I don't wanna fill you fulla parvoviroids?

BLUE: *Shit on this virus mumbo!* What you don't want. Is *me*. A human being on your hands who might feel pain. Or make a demand. Or need you in her guts when there's nothing left.

(Beat)

TORCH: That! Is totally. And complete. *Bullshit!*

BLUE: Torch, I didn't risk my life to come here for a *visit*! I came to live with you, maybe even to die with you. I didn't know what I'd find. Would your skin be smooth and white, like before, or would you be covered with sores? I didn't know. And I didn't care.

(Beat)

TORCH: *(Pleading)* Blue—

BLUE: I know. It's like I said. *(Turns to ascend stairs to entrance door.)* You're a pussy.

TORCH: *(Springing to his feet)* You eat that!

BLUE: Die alone.

(He crosses quickly and grabs her.)

(A significant beat as he looks into her face, makes his decision, then flings her back onto mattress.)

TORCH: All right. Take off your dress.

BLUE: You take it off.

(He rips the dress from her body and grabs her between the legs.)

TORCH: You talk pretty hot for such a dry hole!

BLUE: You man enough to get it wet?

TORCH: Maybe I don't *care* if it's wet.

BLUE: Hey! Use the *palm* of your hand! What am I, a video game?

TORCH: Oh, so *now* you're gonna tell me how to give satisfaction!

BLUE: You gotta tell men everything!

TORCH: There ain't gonna be no love in this, Blue!

BLUE: *Love?* You hide behind it, anyway.

TORCH: I'm a loaded gun, Blue!

BLUE: So shoot me!

TORCH: I got poison fangs, Blue!

BLUE: So bite me!

TORCH: There's *death* in this, Blue!

(Beat, as they stare into each other's eyes.)

(She grasps him by the back of the neck and draws him down to her for a long, deep kiss. They begin making love as:)

(The lights dim.)

CURTAIN

FORTY-DEUCE

FORTY-DEUCE opened in workshop at the Perry Street Theater in New York City on 20 February 1981. It was produced by Steven Steinlauf, with the following cast and creative contributors:

AUGIE . . . . John Seitz
MITCHELL . . . . Thomas Waites
RICKY . . . . .Barry Miller
CRANK . . . . .Willie Reale
BLOW . . . . .John Pankow
JOHN ANTHONY . . . . Timothy Mathias
ROPER . . . . William Hunt

Director . . . . .Sheldon Larry

FORTY-DEUCE reopened at the same theater on 11 October 1981. It was produced by Steven Steinlauf and Anne Thomson, with the following cast and creative contributors:

AUGIE . . . . Harris Laskawy
MITCHELL . . . . Ahvi Spindell
RICKY . . . . Kevin Bacon
CRANK . . . . .Tommy Citera
BLOW . . . . .Mark Keyloun
JOHN ANTHONY . . . . .John Noonan
ROPER . . . . Orson Bean

Director . . . . Tony Tanner

The author wishes to thank Michael Cristofer for his invaluable assistance in editing the script.

For John Paul Hudson and Ed Kruse

"...these torture rooms of the living idiom."

CHARACTERS & SETTING

AUGIE, *Brooklyn Italian, in his forties*
MITCHELL, *Manhattan Jewish, in his late teens*
RICKY, *Brooklyn Italian, in his late teens*
CRANK, *Brooklyn Italian, in his late teens*
BLOW, *Lower East Side Ukrainian, in his late teens*
JOHN ANTHONY, *WASP, in his early teens*
ROPER, *WASP, about fifty years old*

ACT ONE

Scene One: Afternoon
Scene Two: A short while later

ACT TWO

Scene One: Night
Scene Two: A few moments later

TIME

The present

SETTING

The environs of Times Square, a Sunday in the middle of a suffocating August in New York City

A single set: a dingy room overlooking Eighth Avenue. A few sticks of battered furniture—chairs, a table—including, against the back wall, a bureau with peeling mirror. A disproportionately large unmade bed, possibly tilted downstage, so that a nude body, curved and twisted upon it, is made the visual focus throughout. It is a conventional hotel room, with entrance door, bathroom door, and window, its aged crinkled shade half drawn.

Note: The dialogue's orthography and punctuation, if occasionally unorthodox, is deliberate. A glossary is provided at the end of the play.

ACT ONE

Scene One

(The curtain rises on JOHN ANTHONY, *nude on the bed, his slender form twisted in sleep.)*

(The murky yellow light of a hot New York City summer afternoon glows through the open window. There are the occasional rumble of the subway and low traffic sounds throughout.)

(Out of the open bathroom doorway there sticks a naked human foot, big, broad, and dirty, twitching on the floor.)

(Enter AUGIE *through the entrance door, after we hear a rasping of keys in the automatic lock. He pauses by the bed and stares at the boy asleep upon it.)*

AUGIE: Jeez. Fuckin' jeez.

(He bends over the bed, peering more intently at JOHN ANTHONY, *who remains sleeping.)*

AUGIE: Up the fuckin' ass. Off the wall and up the fuckin' ass.

(He shakes the boy. The boy does not wake.)

AUGIE: You better not be for Chrissakes dead. Hey, fuck nuts, I'm talking to you.

(The foot sticking from the open bathroom doorway twitches violently. Slowly MITCHELL *sits up and leans out.)*

MITCHELL: Augie? God, Augie, she's shitface.

AUGIE: *(To* MITCHELL*)* How's from this twerp?

MITCHELL: *(Referring to himself)* Shitface I tell you. Been to breakfast with a shrankroid? *(He starts crawling towards* AUGIE.*)*

AUGIE: Did I ask you a question, bitch?

MITCHELL: We was holin' some shit, me and Crank and Ricky? Some shit you would never know it was dope.

*(*AUGIE *crosses to a chair by the window, stepping over* MITCHELL. AUGIE *sits, his legs spread, hands dangling ominously between them.)*

AUGIE: Did I fuckin' ask you a fuckin' question you cock suck you mother suck?

(MITCHELL *has crawled to the bed. He raises himself to sit on the bed's margin.*)

MITCHELL: You know how sometimes when it's good you rush like....
(His hands rise in a geiser motion.) Woooooooooooosh: *puff! (On the last syllable, his fingertips delicately explode.)* Well, this was like.... *(The geiser motion again)* Wooooooooooosh: *blat! (On last syllable, he makes a loud, flatulent noise.)*

AUGIE: The twerp. On the bed.

MITCHELL: Oh sure. Her too. Ricky snatched her off a Greyhound.
(He looks around, under bed.) Purse's here somewhere. Got a cigarette?

AUGIE: Fuckin' bozo queen bozo fuck.

(He stands abruptly up. MITCHELL reacts. AUGIE crosses to window.)

AUGIE: That guinea testicle I leave in charge? *(He sends window shade flapping up. Looks out)* Creepy fuckin' steambath Eighth Avenue at... *(Looks at watch)* At three-thirty Sunday afternoon. Up the fuckin' ass out the window on the fuckin' street. Jeez.

*(MITCHELL *locates his bag under bed. Removes a brush from it, crosses to bureau.*)*

MITCHELL: You should of been here Saturday night. *(He looks into mirror. Begins brushing hair.)* I seen this dogfight. A coupla German Shepherds belong to these two blind spades workin' the same corner? *(He begins goofing into the mirror.)* "Watch yo' ass, nigger, this here *my* turf." "Let the *dogs* decide, sucker." And those Shepherds, Augie, they was cock- suckin' two of the *nastiest* girls on Forty-deuce. I *mean*? Usually dogs got the big watery eyes go, you know, "twenny-five cents, thirty-five cents, make it fifty"? Shit, they rip out your pussy. Such a scene. And nobody, you know? Nobody give a ka-fuck. Twenny million niggers and spics, ten million dope fiends, forty truckloads of faggots from New Jersey, two hunnert thousand hookers and six stupid cops. Augie. Listen. I need a vacation. It's hard on a Jewish queen. *(Goofing again.)* "Wanna fuck?" "Wanna get high?" "Wanna suck fuck toke poke peel feel and get *numb*?" Dope and sex and dope and sex and dope. Augie, you come up with the third kick I marry you?

AUGIE: You come up with Ricky I break your arm.

*(MITCHELL *ceases brushing hair.*)*

MITCHELL: OK. I think he's in the bat'room. *(Pause)* Asleep on the toilet?

*(AUGIE *continues gazing out the window.*)*

AUGIE: *(Toneless.)* Asleep on the toilet.

MITCHELL: He passes out on the toilet. I pass out on the bat'room floor. The kid drags it in here, passes out on the bed. Crank don't bat a cocksuckin' eyelash, he just asks which way is the door, and dances.

AUGIE: *(Toneless)* Asleep on the fuckin' toilet.

(MITCHELL crosses to bed, rummages under it, pulls out a pair of high heels.)

MITCHELL: Augie. Don't worry. Money? He's *got* money.

AUGIE: Those new ones I send up here?

(MITCHELL is putting on the high heels.)

MITCHELL: Those rabbis? Jesus, Augie. Plus, I turned one from the Haymarket, but that's mine.

(AUGIE turns from window to face MITCHELL.)

AUGIE: You use this room?

MITCHELL: Sure I use this room. I give Ricky a cut for this room.

AUGIE: You use this room one of your tricks you deal with me.

MITCHELL: And where was you?

AUGIE: None of your asshole. You deal with me or you go fuck all. There's this, and the place on Forty-sixth, and the room across Port Authority. You wanna use the facilities you don't deal with nobody but me.

MITCHELL: I deal with you since I'm on the street.

(AUGIE stares at MITCHELL in silence, then moves from the window to stare into the offstage bathroom. Enters bathroom. A slapping sound can be heard. MITCHELL winces with each slap.)

MITCHELL: *(Continued)* Ka-fuck.

(AUGIE marches a bleary RICKY out of bathroom. Brings him downstage center; and tries to stand him up. RICKY keeps slumping against AUGIE, who slaps the youth's face.)

AUGIE: The money, you little shit. I send two new ones up here.

RICKY: *(Thickly)* What you fuck?

AUGIE: And you put a twelve-year-old to work in my room. You tank up a twelve-year-old put him to work in my facilities.

RICKY: What you fuck?

(He tries to back away from AUGIE, who slaps him.)

AUGIE: Sixteen, that's O K, sixteen, I can handle sixteen. *(Slaps RICKY's face)*

AUGIE: Even maybe say fifteen, I can handle fifteen. *(Slaps RICKY again)*

AUGIE: But how I explain to Mike about twelve? Hey? How I explain this here twelve-year-old to Mike? This ain't no agency operation, you testicle. This here is bang-and-walk.

(RICKY slides to the floor.)

AUGIE: You can't work no twelve-year-old outa rooms on the Square. What you think, you workin' for some white man does business over the phone outa some floorthrough Upper East with the Bloomingdale's pillows and rugs and shit? You a greasy little guinea and you workin' for a greaser and I know the rules this fuckin' neighborhood and I say I don't handle no twelve-year-old fags!

(He jerks RICKY's *head up by his hair.)*

AUGIE: Unnerstand?

MITCHELL: Augie. Hey. Listen. I think the message is definitely getting through?

*(*AUGIE *releases* RICKY *and crosses to bed to stand in front of* MITCHELL, *whom he fixes with his finger.)*

AUGIE: You. You wrap up that chickie. You take her over to G G's you tell her to work outa there. What they do in that armpit is their business prob'ly give her a fuckin' trophy or somethin'. Whole lotta street twats dressed up for Christmas anyhow. *(He turns, stares at floor.)* Twelve-year-old hustler bring Mike up my pussy so fuckin' fast I get hemmeroids.

(He crosses to RICKY *and bends over him.)*

AUGIE: Clean up the Square that's what they oughta do, you greaseball. You member what went down all them niggers runnin' the twelve-year-old white chicks? Well, that ain't gonna happen my facilities no fuckin' way. *(He moves to the chair, sits, his hands dangling between his legs. Vaguely addresses room.)* I lose my protection you bitches have to suck it off in the street. Mike blacklist you every hotel in the Square. *(He begins nodding his head.)* This here is clean, it's quick, and it's guaranteed. *(Pause)* This here is like a Burger King.

*(*RICKY *begins to retch.* MITCHELL *crosses to him.)*

MITCHELL: We didn't oughta hole that ka-fuckin' motor oil. *(Strokes* RICKY's *head)* Don't you feel shittier'n shit? *(Addresses* AUGIE*)* You want I should get some coffee that bodega downstairs?

AUGIE: *(To* RICKY*)* The money, greaseball.

MITCHELL: *(To* RICKY*)* Hey. The man wants the rent. Let's put you on the bed. That's right. Up we go.

(He helps RICKY *to his feet and crosses with him to the bed.* RICKY *sits on the bed's right margin.)*

MITCHELL: Hey. You want I should get us some coffee? Ricky? *(Addresses* JOHN ANTHONY's *slumbering body)* Hey. Move over. *(Shakes* JOHN ANTHONY, *who stirs, comes to stupefied life, sits up, looks about wild and unseeing, and rolls over to lie on his stomach.)*

RICKY: *(Thickly)* Buncha twenny dollar tricks up your ass twenny dollar tricks.

AUGIE: You don't like the action you can fuck off—go back East New York. Know what I mean?

RICKY: I got a deal goin' you look cheap standing next to it.

AUGIE: You owe me, greaseball. You owe me from last night. You fuckin' owe me from two weeks ago.

RICKY: These two niggers, one is a dyke. She has a whole lotta blow. This one's buying into it.

AUGIE: So?

RICKY: This one's investing.

AUGIE: So?

RICKY: This one is copping.

AUGIE: So?

RICKY: So I taste it. So it's uncut. So I pay you back.

AUGIE: You owe me, greaseball. I put you in charge, you fuck up.

RICKY: I turn those two yids you send up here. That your idea of trade—two fuckin' bearded yids?

MITCHELL: They was *weird*, Augie. Like straight outa *shul*. I thought they was gonna pray over us.

AUGIE: *(To RICKY)* Kike money, nigger money, what you fuckin' care?

RICKY: Tried to get away with fifteen. You tell them fifteen, you fuck.

AUGIE: So you service both at once. That's thirty.

RICKY: My asshole.

(There is banging at the door. MITCHELL moves to entrance door and admits CRANK.)

CRANK: Mitchell? Was that shit shit?

MITCHELL: Could'a died, you syphilis.

CRANK: Hey. Augie.

AUGIE: Crank. Money.

CRANK: Ricky and me we got this operation we pay you later? Hey. Ricky. *(He approaches bed; looks down at RICKY.)*

AUGIE: *(To CRANK)* I own these facilities. I fuckin' own *you* from last week. Any tricks get turned, any dope trade hands, I get my commission. Ricky tells me he such a testicle he deal with some jig dyke got fancy stuff. You the other testicle?

CRANK: *(To* RICKY*)* Some mother shit, wadn't it? Augie. There's this dyke—her old man? Says he'll front us. Last night we party? Only I use this shit offa Blow.

MITCHELL: Crank, you want I should go get some coffee?

RICKY: Five C's, Augie. All we need is five C's. The niggers front us the rest.

CRANK: I can cut it, carry it, like in two hours?

AUGIE: Where these niggers get this blow?

CRANK: Fuck if I know. But the mothers is close, Augie. Real close. Only they gotta move fast. By tonight.

AUGIE: Why some niggers front you fuck? Two goddamn queers.

RICKY: *(To* CRANK*)* You listen to her? Every hooker use this room she say push the milk sugar. Every East Side bitch every New Jersey twat every cheap Toyota cruisin' Third Avenue. She knows faggots snort coke like...

MITCHELL: Like it was gonna make their cocks grow.

CRANK: 'Cept for them schmucks last night? Jesus. The fuzzy one in the dumb hat? He don't even take it off.

RICKY: Augie's the fuckin' Jew. He don't want no competition. Crappy milk sugar act all excited so suckin' cheap.

AUGIE: *(To* RICKY*)* You commission me, you nigger. Mike don't go for no independent action.

RICKY: Mike don't have to know.

AUGIE: Where a little greaser like you get a slice of any kind of anything?

RICKY: That midtown three-piece with the silver wig? He pay plenty for that fetus. *(He jerks his thumb at* JOHN ANTHONY, *behind him.)*

*(*AUGIE *abruptly rises.)*

AUGIE: You mean Roper? You goin' for Roper? You nose into my contacts I cut it off. I stuff it up your big flappin' asshole.

RICKY: Too late. He's innerested.

AUGIE: Roper is very upper class, Ricky. Very...upper...class.

MITCHELL: I know that number. Weird? Blow and me once we see him comm outa Sixth Avenue. You ready for this? *(Gestures)* Blow cocksuckin' *waves.*

CRANK: And the john fuckin' waves back, right?

*(*AUGIE *is still on his feet, staring at* RICKY.*)*

AUGIE: Roper's Mike's special. Likes a production. (*Points at* RICKY.) Mike burn your ass he find out. (*He sits abruptly down; hands fidget between his legs.*) Copping Mike's special. Jeez. Fuckin' jeez.

RICKY: Mike ain't gonna know. Augie, think with your fuckin' head. Some little creep like third rate numbers runner like cheapo bagman sittin on *your* face. We gotta open this up or we gonna get old and yellow you and me and Crank like the stains on these sheets. (*He stands; crosses to* AUGIE.) Roper don't care fuck. He play, you bring the ball. That little kid is a goddam virgin. Stone him he'll do anything won't know from shit.

AUGIE: Jeez.

(CRANK *reaches across bed; shakes* JOHN ANTHONY.)

CRANK: Hey. John Anthony.

MITCHELL: (*To* CRANK) She stinks, don't she?

CRANK: How the fuck I know she stink?

MITCHELL: Long bus ride from ka-fucking nowhere.

(JOHN ANTHONY *jerks suddenly to life, sits up, stares with great eyes ringed, unseeing, burning, straight at audience. Then he plops sideways and curls into a ball in the middle of the bed.*)

RICKY: (*To* AUGIE.) Roper he comes by later. All hotted up and cash in his pants.

AUGIE: Fuckin' jeez.

(RICKY *suddenly grips his belly; returns to bed, sitting next to* CRANK.)

RICKY: What was *in* that shit?

MITCHELL: (*Generally*) Want I should go get some coffee?

CRANK: So Mitchell. Ditn't you turn one last night?

MITCHELL: I give a dime to Blow, I shoot last night's on three cards.

CRANK: Three cards?

MITCHELL: Red black black red. This dealer he had his old lady along and are you ready? She hadda kid in this baby carriage standin' right next to the Monte table. I could vomit it was so cheap. Fucks your timing all to fuck. You thinkin', I win and I take the Gerbers from this black brat. Now is that cheap?

CRANK: Woulda fucked *my* timing, Mitchell.

AUGIE: (*To* RICKY) O K, greaseball. Get this. Thirty percent. By tomorrow morning not a speck of nigger coke in these facilities.

CRANK: Thirty! That leaves...that leaves what?

RICKY: Enough. *(To* AUGIE.*)* O K, you fuckin' bloodsucker.

AUGIE: Mike find out, I'm dead. So what does that mean, bloodsucker?

MITCHELL: That bodega downstairs. Four coffees. Regular? Xtra light? Light?

*(*AUGIE *rummages for change.)*

AUGIE: Fuck them spics. Go to the corner Forty-fifth. The Greeks.

MITCHELL: They charge twice as much the Greeks.

*(*RICKY *is in evident pain, his head bowed.)*

RICKY: Money suckin' Greek bastards everywhere you look. Charge you a dollar for a glass of water. *(To* MITCHELL*)* Carton of milk.

*(*AUGIE *gives money to* MITCHELL.*)*

AUGIE: The Greeks. Xtra light. Take Ricky's keys.

RICKY: A carton of milk. The bodega. Crank. Give her the money.

*(*CRANK *draws crumpled bills from jeans; hands to* MITCHELL.*)*

CRANK: The bodega.

MITCHELL: What am I, gonna go downstairs for you corner Forty-fifth for Augie? What am I?

*(*RICKY *begins speaking in gasps, head bowed.)*

RICKY: Fuckin' Greeks eighty-five cents for a Diet-Rite four dollars for a lousy pancake. Fuckin' Greeks fuckin' mothers. They come over here make a few bucks offa hot cigarettes souvlaki sandwiches. Buy up every shit corner this town. You can't get a fuckin' cup of coffee 'tween Forty-two and Fifty, Eight over to Five, some Greek don't charge you up the rectum. Orange juice? A lousy pint of orange juice the Greeks make you drop your pants. Push out all the bodegas shoot up the prices take over the Square. Screw the numbers people, the peddlers, the loose joints, the hookers, charge us up the pee-hole pack pieces under their big fat cash register smiles you walk in. Send the fuckers back to Astoria piss on their two by four lawns.

AUGIE: O K, O K. The bodega.

MITCHELL: That's big of you, Augie, know what I mean?

AUGIE: The coffee, you yo-yo.

MITCHELL: Xtra light! Crank, you want light? Ricky, a carton of milk. What about the kid?

RICKY: Milk for him too. A toasted corn. Or a bran, toasted, with orange marmalade.

MITCHELL: Orange marmalade?

RICKY: Or a English.

AUGIE: A glass'a egg cream. Take the edge off the breath 'tween her legs.

MITCHELL: And bring down her price? (*Exits through entrance door after snatching* RICKY's *keys*)

AUGIE: (*To* RICKY) Thirty plus my commission last night. Two at fifteen—one at twenny.

RICKY: What fuckin' one at twenny?

AUGIE: (*Meaning* MITCHELL) That Jew bitch turn one these facilities. That's all mine. I leave you in charge it's just a fuckin' favor. Jeez. Give him a piece greaseball thinks it's Christmas. Thinks he's runnin' things. Dumb little guinea with the big head. (*Deliberately*) Guinea fuck up I got no choice.

RICKY: It's in the pocket.

(*There is a quick tapping at the door.* CRANK *crosses to door and admits* BLOW, *a package under his arm.*)

BLOW: (*To* CRANK) Hey. I just see Mitchell? I get eat out by this Long Island—tells me about his wife. Augie. Where was you last night? Asshole looks Wall Street his shoes to his dyed hair. Wears these forty dollar faded jeans. Wants me to talk dirty? For him the Dixie Hotel is slumming. His underwear is bleached? Sniffs my pits and makes a face. Fuck I wash this morning.

AUGIE: (*To* BLOW) We got three testicles this fuckin' deal?

BLOW: What fuckin' three? What deal?

RICKY: (*To* BLOW) You poison me, you shit.

CRANK: Blow, you poison Ricky.

BLOW: (*To* RICKY) Hey. You geeze that scum? I ditn't know you geeze that scum.

CRANK: What else?

BLOW: I front you that scum.

AUGIE: You a third testicle, Blow? The niggers all this fancy-ass coke?

BLOW: I don't know from Ricky's deals. I don't work for you, Augie.

AUGIE: (*Toneless*) You don't work for me.

BLOW: Maybe I turn a trick here. Maybe you get a piece of that. But I don't hang out here, Augie.

AUGIE: Blow, you don't work for me, you don't work for nobody, right?

BLOW: I sell dick I sell dope. I come I go.

AUGIE: You come you go. I don't own your asshole, right? So why is your fuckin' asshole in my facilities?

BLOW: Augie. Last night I drop off some shit. It's discount, know what I mean? You wanna piece of that? Ricky say fuck yes he can handle it. So I front him. Only the dumb shit pokes it up his arm.

RICKY: You front me my fuckin' ass. Scrape it outa pussy some Ninth Avenue transie.

BLOW: So how's the kid?

RICKY: So what's the kid to you?

BLOW: I talk to that kid last night. Told him, hey, I bring you a present.

RICKY: That kid don't need presents from no fuckin' bohunk. That kid is my business.

BLOW: Hey. You watch it with him?

RICKY: What you fuck?

BLOW: He don't get hurt. Easy up?

CRANK: Ricky say, Roper's the one.

BLOW: Roper.

CRANK: We got plans?

BLOW: Crank, you crazy you throw that kid at Roper. I know Roper. I do Roper. He's fuckin' Upper East.

CRANK: We got plans. Ricky?

RICKY: I go into the bat'room. I put my face in a sink of water. I come out. There is nobody's bohunk nose in my business. *(He rises painfully, crosses to bathroom, enters and slams the door.)*

AUGIE: *(Loudly)* That was O K. I mean he's sick and all but that was O K. *(Normal voice)* Hot shit greaser.

CRANK: *(To BLOW)* You really buy him a present?

(BLOW ignores CRANK and crosses to bed.)

BLOW: Hey. John Anthony. *(He kneels on bed.)* Look what I brung you. *(He undoes package.)* You said, you saw this T-shirt? I said, but it's tacky? You said, yeah, but you was gonna buy it. *(He shows the T-shirt; it has the words "New York City" and an apple printed on it.)* I got it small cause you so fuckin' little.

CRANK: *(To AUGIE)* Ricky and me, it's a hunnert percent sure thing?

AUGIE: Testicle.

CRANK: It works, and then we got a operation?

AUGIE: Not in my facilities. This a one-shot on account Mike can't know. I shouldn't taken off last night.

BLOW: *(To* JOHN ANTHONY.*)* Like I was sayin' before, maybe we team up. I take you over to the Haymarket, introduce you? Gotta hang out somewhere. *(He lowers his voice.)* This a rip, kid.

CRANK: Hey. Maybe we deal with Mike?

AUGIE: Testicle. You deal with me you deal with Mike.

CRANK: O.K. We deal with you we deal with Mike.

BLOW: Hey. I brung you this tacky bullshit shirt. *(He lowers his voice.)* Come on, kid. Wake the fuck up.

AUGIE: I get this operation by fuckin' with Mike's specials? Mike you know where Mike is comin' from? You save me trouble, I cut you in. You make me trouble, I cut you out. Eight, ten operations he got to have managers. Run here run fuck. He got no time. And time, you testicle, that is the reason for everything.

BLOW: *(Low tones)* I come back for you later? *(He begins stroking* JOHN ANTHONY*'s hair.)*

CRANK: Time? Augie?

AUGIE: Time means I can do this and that and fuck it I move free don't answer to nobody. So what you got the East Sixties floorthrough and a condo in the Hamptons! You got to do this for that one and see her and bend over for this one and suck the other one's hole. You maybe get paid good but you still a fuckin' whore. You take Roper.

BLOW: *(To* CRANK*)* Hey. Is the kid sick?

CRANK: We all sick that slime you feed us.

BLOW: *(Jerking round)* You shoot him with that?

CRANK: I shoot the room, I shoot myself. Augie?

AUGIE: Consultant she calls herself. Oil companies. Plastics. Big cocksuckin' deal. Anyhow she sittin' hunnerth floor Sixth Avenue with a big ugly bone on. Or they fuckin' send her to Houston where she can't even cross her fuckin' legs. She tell me once, in New York they deliver the goods. Bitch goes to Paris, to It'ly, to fuckin' Africa. She say, only New York. In New York, she say, kicks? They let you run up a tab, bill you quarterly. Saves you time. On the mother *street*. Tell *her* about time.

BLOW: *(Low tones)* Don't never do no shit these here numbers, know what I mean?

AUGIE: With guys like Roper you gotta know the fuck you doin. You don't say, hey. I got this twelve-year-old stashed up Eighth Avenue. Fresh off the suckin' bus. Sure she show up lickin her lips. Cause she know she dealin' with amateurs. It could be dangerous. It fires her ass. But something go wrong she don't complain to you. She go to Mike. She can't come. Hey? Or the kid he get hurt. Or she gets her tits in a wringer. Or maybe some undercover cocksuck has add it up for hisself follow her up here. The bitch get scared Mike gotta fix. Then where you are? Testicle! People keep trippin' over this big smelly fat kid dead in the street.

BLOW: *(Low tones)* Bastards. Would I put a spike through that skin?

(RICKY emerges from the bathroom towelling his face. He glares at the two on the bed.)

CRANK: Hey. Ricky. We got a operation?

RICKY: *(Eyes on bed)* What else?

AUGIE: Dumb ass greaser. I got this operation fuckin' with Mike?

RICKY: *(Eyes on bed)* This turkey room is no operation.

(On the bed, BLOW begins tentatively stroking JOHN ANTHONY's body.)

AUGIE: Mike now he knows. Got his fingers up bitches like Roper. Did Mike ever give out with the real fuckin' thing? Tank up some slut offa Fifty-third maybe. Say she such a virgin you could eat outa her jockstrap hand her to Roper does *that* bitch know or fuckin' care? Bitches like Roper they come Forty-deuce offa fucking Madison Ave, offa fuckin' Lex. They think the shit on the floor is outa some movie. Like them Roper bitches is innocent, you nigger. They used to pickin' up phones and pressin' buttons. They order outa some catalog. Hooker flops out with the rubber-plated tits flashbulbs 'tween his legs disco music screamin' out his asshole. Control. You got to control every shit detail you deal with guys like that.

RICKY: *(Eyes on bed)* Every cheap shot this town scared somebody gonna grab a little.

(BLOW stiffens suddenly on the bed.)

BLOW: Hey.

AUGIE: Down to the minute. Guys like that they fuckin' cream on a schedule so tight you better be sure nothin' interfere. Control, you greaser. Control.

RICKY: *(To BLOW)* What you fuck?

BLOW: He's cacked.

(RICKY crosses at once to the bed. Pushes BLOW to one side and bends over JOHN ANTHONY, feeling for his pulse.)

BLOW: Is this for real? Cacked?

(Enter MITCHELL, with paper bag, through door after rasping of lock.)

MITCHELL: Coffee wagon! So will you line up, girls? (*He begins taking each item out of sack and placing it on bureau.*)

(RICKY *drops* JOHN ANTHONY's *wrist and covers his mouth with his hand. Everyone except* MITCHELL *is frozen.*)

MITCHELL:. Xtra light for Augie? Regular is for me, and does she need this danish? Light for Crank. Ricky? Carton of milk. Nothing for you, Blow, you eat my dime you suck dick. A toasted corn, Ricky. No bran. And marmalade I ask you does a P R know from marmalade? I go, Hey mon. Lay a little grape jelly on the dried-up thing. He looks at me. I go, So mash up a fuckin' fried banana or something don't leave it all crusty like a goddamned scab? He looks at me. I go, Besides two boxes Uncle Ben's white rice, a can of peaches, seven Hershey bars and cigarettes, what the fuck you got in this store? (*Pause*) You know?

(*No one responds.* AUGIE *crosses quickly to bed, slips his hand under the boy's chest, stares wildly, then sinks to bed's margin, head in hands.*)

AUGIE: Fuckin' jeez.

MITCHELL: (*Looking from one to the other.*) Hey. You want I should go back? (*Pause*) Ricky? (*Pause. He uses his fingers to itemize.*) Xtra light. (*Pause*) Light. (*Pause*) A carton of fuckin' milk. (*Pause*) And a toasted corn. (*Pause*) Hey. Does a P R know from marmalade?

(*Silence+*)

(*Lights down*)

Scene Two

(*A short while later.* MITCHELL's *consignment of plastic cups is scattered now about the floor; as aimlessly as the characters themselves.*)

(*A sheet has been hastily thrown over* JOHN ANTHONY's *body, but his feet and an outstretched arm, fingers curled, are still visible.*)

(*The window shade is fully drawn now, but* AUGIE *has turned back an edge and is peering down into the street. He is ominously silent.* RICKY *sits backwards in a chair, looking at* AUGIE. CRANK *squats on the floor between them, glancing furtively from one to the other.* BLOW *sits on the bed's left margin, staring at the wall.* MITCHELL *is half-supine on the floor; propped against the bed's foot, his long legs, capped in heels, thrown out before him. He is meditatively munching a danish.*)

MITCHELL: Hey. Maybe we set fire to this fuckin' building? Who would know from just another body all burn to a crisp? Just last week right on Forty-two. Hey Blow you was there.

(BLOW *does not respond.*)

MITCHELL: All them hookers in the massage parlor hangin out the third story. Everybody on the street yellin Fire, ya dumb bitches! The whole top three floors is on fuckin' fire. Girls so stoned they start carrying on you know hangin' out the windows with the wigs and the tits figure the fire is good for business? So who woulda know coupla girls check out in that one you think anybody ask questions? *(Pause)* Hey. The only time I see a dead body was my grandmother? Such a drunk my grandmother. I never see her since I'm like fifteen? For a Jew my old man was not family-orientated. We live East Side, my grandmother was way the fuck on Staten Island? Coulda been Florida all my dad care. Only time I'm on Staten Island was the bitch's funeral. Ka-fuck. My dad. *(Pause)* Italian neighborhood. Italians are very into funerals. Very family-orientated. Hey. Crank's Italian. Crank. Italians you know what I mean?

(CRANK *does not respond.*)

MITCHELL: There was this whole building Sixty-second and First—practically give birth to our building Sixty-fifth and Second? All the old grandmothers—big deal every Sunday. Guineas and Jews and spics are up the ka-pussy with family. Only my people, even when I got a grandmother she lives way the fuck on Staten Island? *(Pause)* It wadn't easy a big Jewish queen Italian neighborhood. Coulda been worse, I know. Coulda been Boro Park. *(Pause)* But I was a hitter. *(Pause)* Anglo neighborhoods black neighborhoods now they don't care so fuckin' much. Anglo guys my neighborhood was goin' to college you know what I mean? Some queen was just local color. But you watch it with guineas. I don't even trust a faggot if he's Italian. Or Spanish? Ricky will tell you these Italians. Hey. Ricky.

(RICKY *does not respond.*)

MITCHELL: My ka-fucking dad. I wear these hot pants once for the big fag crusade up Christopher every year? Pink hot pants ride up my thighs you could see my balls. Said I jiggled like the fringe on a chenille bedspread. You think he give a shit? All the time tanked to the tits, he just hope I ain't givin' no blow jobs to no shvartzers? Ditn't want his kid goin' down on no shvartzers. Only the goyim he says. He says, all that pink skin and clean hair how could they give you disease? My dad. *(Pause)* But you know sometimes I think goyim are the worst. You take a spic—now O K maybe he get mean. But if he got a bone on he fuck you up the ass, call it pussy, what the hell? But goyim they just look at you like you wadn't there or like the street was a movie and you was this extra? *(Pause)* But my dad—

AUGIE: *(Exploding)* Fuck your fuckin' dad! *(Finger rigidly extended, he turns to confront RICKY.)* So guinea you got it figured yet? You know what it cost move that dead cunt some place make it look like a accident? Know who you gotta deal with? The one them two niggers is comin' here to rip. The one what owns Roper's business. I say, hey Mike there this dead chicken in

the Eighth Avenue apartment? With two niggers sellin' non-regulation shit
to this uppity little greaser? What has his thumb up the twat one of your
superspecial customers. So, Mike, hey. Can you fix it for me? *(Pause)*
So, fuck nuts. You got it figured yet?

RICKY: I send Crank to tell the niggers.

AUGIE: Oh yeah right. And they go, Oh yeah sure that's O K we catch you
next week.

RICKY: Only to come later. The deal is bigger now.

AUGIE: What?

RICKY: To come later. It take awhile now with Roper.

AUGIE: Yeah it take like the rest of your fuckin' life. Mike just make a phone
call and greaser here can tell it to the Mid-town Precinct. They get here just
in time to catch your act. *(He strides to bed, throws back the sheet.)* So what am
I bid for this chicken. Hey? Here this stupid greaser queer tryin' to sell this
skinny corpse to some uptown number who maybe can't tell when the trade
is alive but who fuckin' knows a dead whore when he sees one. *(He begins
furiously turning the body about.)* So what am I bid? Here's a foot fulla five
stiff toes. Fifty cents. Here's a vein got a track so big you could run your
cock half way up her arm. Dollar fifty? Do I hear two? Ever see a mouth like
that give you a blow job for days. Asshole tight as a drum butt like a rubber
pad stick clamps on it. Scissor off her nipples wire her up and make her
move. Wire her hands to her ankles her knee to her neck and her cock to her
belly her foot to her mouth her neck bent back jerk and jiggle when you
spread her legs—

(BLOW turns, reaches across bed and grips AUGIE's wrist.)

BLOW: That is a fuckin' dead body! *(AUGIE stares at BLOW.)*

BLOW: There is a dead kid here? *(Pause)*

AUGIE: Let go my arm you bohunk, you testicle.

(BLOW releases AUGIE.)

AUGIE: And leave us not forget who killed this fetus. This fetus was caved in
by a lotta poison dope offa this twenny-five cent Uke called Blow.

*(BLOW turns and sinks onto bed again. AUGIE throws sheet carelessly over body
and returns to window. He peers out.)*

AUGIE: What the fuck you mean, tell the niggers later?

RICKY: You can kill my ass, or Mike can kill my ass, what else can I do but
use the kid if he's cacked or he's not? I got two ugly niggers kill my ass you
don't. I gotta make that deal and that kid is my only way. Roper pay plenty
he think he kill that kid. I tell you five C's? Roper pay fuckin' five G's he

think he kill the kid. We tell the niggers, come later. They'll bite—for five fat ones.

AUGIE: *(Peering out window)* Big head on a little greaser. You talkin' a tricky fuckin' operation.

RICKY: You can kill my ass, Augie, or maybe you can leave it to Mike. Or them niggers can kill my ass. It don't matter a shit to me, Augie, it don't. *(Pause)*

CRANK: It don't matter a shit to Ricky, Augie.

(AUGIE slowly turns from the window. Glares at CRANK)

RICKY: Shut the fuck up, Crank.

AUGIE: *(To CRANK)* I tell Mike to kill the fat faggot first. I tell him to hang the fat fag by her big tits from the West Side Highway. *(Pause) (To RICKY)* O K, big head. Let's say you pull it off with Mrs. Roper. You still got this body stinkin' up my bed.

RICKY: Mike take care of that body. Who else?

AUGIE: How Mike take care of that body? Mike take care of that body he kill your ass.

RICKY: Maybe. Maybe not. It was some john cacked the kid. You ditn't know. I ditn't know. Roper he's not talkin'. It was some john outa the Haymarket. Mike get rid of dead whores before.

AUGIE: Roper tell Mike.

RICKY: Why he want Mike to know? He's enough trouble we know.

AUGIE: This a tricky fuckin' operation, greaseball. Roper gonna spring for a dead whore?

RICKY: Roper ain't gonna know. I say, the kid's so stoned he's out of it Mr Roper you can do whatever. Now Roper is out of it too, know what I mean? Dust.

AUGIE: Roper don't get dusted.

RICKY: Roper get dusted today. *(Pause)* So O K, maybe Roper ties the kid up—some weird shit. Maybe even tries to cut him a little—what the fuck? The kid is already dead, know what I mean? And Roper, Roper can't handle dust. I give him a few minutes. I come back, you know, I forget somethin'. Hey. I do this thing. Hey. What the fuck? The kid you know what I mean looks weird. Hey. Hey. Mr Roper. Hey. Jesus. Oh Jesus... The kid is dead. Roper can't handle dust. *(Pause)*

AUGIE: You are some kinna somethin', greaseball.

RICKY: Then Roper gotta come across. Five fat G's.

AUGIE: How you know I don't call Mike, tell him there this greaser motherfuck got big plans middle of Mike's own fuckin' operation?

RICKY: Mike don't give you piddle shit, hey Augie? And you sick of it. Hey? *(Pause)* That why you gone last night? Saturday night is rip time. *(Pause)* Mike think I fuck him over he think *you* fuck him over. He maybe believe you you kill my ass. But you ain't killed nobody yet and you fuckin' ain't gonna kill me now. *(Pause)*

AUGIE: Half.

RICKY: One fuckin' third.

AUGIE: Half.

RICKY: One fuckin' third. Me. You. And Crank cause he do deliveries.

AUGIE: *(Nodding towards bed)* What about them two?

RICKY: *(Loudly)* Blow keeps his mouth shut he fuckin' peddles funerals. He end up dead too the street find out. Maybe we be nice to him let him carry a little.

(BLOW does not respond.)

RICKY: And Mitchell she hangs out with us. Hey. Mitchell. You hang out with us?

MITCHELL: I hang out with you since I'm sellin' my pussy.

AUGIE: *(Peering out window)* Fuckin' jeez.

RICKY: *(To AUGIE)* I got no choice my ass is dead all kinds of people. Only I think maybe if it's my ass it's your ass too. And his. And hers. And his. *(Pause)*

AUGIE: Midnight.

RICKY: You can't wait the fuck till morning?

AUGIE: Midnight. *(Pause)* I come back at midnight. There's no coke there's no niggers. Just that stiff on the bed and my commission. I ain't been here all day. Settin' up a act. *(Turns from window; to RICKY)* You was in charge. I tell Mike, Ricky was in charge. Then *you* tell him that cocksuck story some john outa the Haymarket. *(Pause)* I ain't been this apartment.

RICKY: I handle Mike.

CRANK: But gotta cut it. Wrap it. Deliver it. By midnight, Ricky?

RICKY: Shut your fuck. *(Pause)*

AUGIE: Jeez. *(Pause)* Midnight. *(He crosses to door. Scans room)* I ain't been these facilities. *(He exits through entrance door.)*

CRANK: (*To* RICKY) That mother is got shit runnin' down his leg he so scared. Ricky? You scared him he got shit runnin' down his leg.

RICKY: (*Standing*) All I smell is sweat offa you—only you too stupid to be scared. We gotta move. You get your fat ass down to Forty-deuce. Tell them niggers to come later. Like at ten. They bitch? And you say fat five.

CRANK: What if they ain't in that armpit bar? What if they gone uptown?

RICKY: Then you go uptown.

CRANK: Ricky? I don't know from uptown. I never go above Ninety-sixth.

RICKY: Shit. Can you be this fuckin' stupid? Dyke hangs out that chili stand that pizza stand on Hunnert Twenny-fifth.

CRANK: Hunnert Twenny-fifth?

RICKY: On the corner. Right where you get off the subway all them niggers pukin' and shootin'. The I R T.

CRANK: The I R T you mean on the Square?

RICKY: Oh fuck. (*Pause*) Blow. It's that hop house that chili parlor pizza joint what the fuck on Hunnert Twenny-fifth?

(BLOW *continues staring at wall.*)

BLOW: There's a dead kid this apartment, Ricky.

RICKY: Blow. You answer the fuckin' question that dyke her old man.

(BLOW *does not respond.*)

RICKY: And after you answer the question then you get me some grass. Dust it kinna heavy, Blow, so Roper don't know the kid is cacked.

(BLOW *does not respond.*)

RICKY: Blow? (*Crosses to opposite side of bed*) Blow? (*Leans across bed. To* BLOW's *back*) Blow you mother.

BLOW: You hadda fuckin' kill him!

(RICKY *and* BLOW *stare at one another.*)

CRANK: You give us that slime. Hey. Ricky—

BLOW: (*To* CRANK) Up your ass, fat suck! (*Pause*) That kid ditn't do shit to shit. He come here this toilet cause his brother say he just a little queer get outa my house my shitty wife and stupid kids. Some upstate crud, can you just see him?

RICKY: What you fuck?

(BLOW *arranges the sheet over* JOHN ANTHONY; *in so doing he pulls the sheet from under* RICKY's *knee.*)

BLOW: Back off.

(RICKY *stands upright.*)

BLOW: Think he so straight prob'ly take it up the ass. I deal with straight guys they all take it up the ass. Then they go back to the wife and the girlfriend and talk about queers! They climb on toppa some cunt and sweat and shake. They can't come they say, Honey, put your finger up my ass please honey pop my ass. I pop your ass you bozo. I put my dick up your straight pussy so many times your old lady die laughin' she see you with your buns in the air! *(Pause)* I see him his buddies cruisin' B-way every goddamn night. Lookin' for cunt so weird—you know that come from nowhere look with the plaid shirts and the lettermen jackets they don't know it but they look like faggots. I cut one outa the pack—he so lame he say, Hey man know where I can get me some warm pussy? You know you gonna end up on toppa his butt grindin' in to him he squeak and moan like a doll you squeeze it! Then he go back to Utica throw out his little brother the little queer can't live with such a real fuckin' man and his real fuckin' wife and real fuckin' brats—just one big fuckin' T V show. Little brother too pretty too sexy for such a big bullshit stud. Fuck Ricky why you guys nail a spike in that kid's arm? *(Pause)* Ricky? Why you slip a needle in that tissue paper skin all them little blue veins how could you do that? Fuck Ricky how could you do that? *(He fiddles some more with the sheet. Discovers T-shirt among the folds)* Stupid tacky shirt. I get him this tacky motherfuck shirt. *(Pause)*

RICKY: You done yet? You finish with the funeral?

BLOW: You kill him and now you fuck, now you wanna sell him!

RICKY: *Who* kill the kid, Blow? *I* ditn't kill the kid. *You* kill the kid, Blow! So what you fuck I sell his dead ass?

(BLOW *sits on bed, staring at shirt.*)

RICKY: A buncha weird ones this apartment buncha dizzy queens don't you unnerstand? We gotta move. Or we gonna have broken glass rubbed in our eyes. Or maybe we get lucky only a coupla fingers bent back. By midnight we gotta have our shit all wrapped up and ready to deliver! Blow: dust. Crank: the niggers. Unnerstand?

CRANK: Yeah, Ricky.

BLOW: Shit.

RICKY: Unnerstand?

BLOW: Fuck O K. I unnerstand! *(Pause)*

RICKY: O K. I'm gonna go into the bat'room. I will *not* be takin a shit. We gotta have a schedule you queens drivin' me crazy. Blow. One hour. Crank. I give you 'til five. The rest of the schedule when I got it figured. You better both be here when I say. *(He crosses to bathroom door, enters, closes door.)*

MITCHELL: *(Looking at door)* Is that gonna be headquarters?

CRANK: Mitchell, how I get to Hunnert Twenny-fifth?

BLOW: It's Hunnert Ten. You come up the subway. Dyke's inna donut shop see her through the plate glass. *(He stands up. Carefully folds T-shirt and places it on bed)* Mitchell, you be here to watch the kid, right?

MITCHELL: She goin' somewhere? Yeah I be here—where else?

BLOW: Keep the sheet over him he's naked?

MITCHELL: Such a father thing you got, Blow. Every twelve-year-old dump her ass on Forty-deuce Blow gotta listen to the big tragedy. Put his arm around her shoulders. Bring her T H C and franks from Nedick's—get what I mean—and then before you know it he's fuckin' her.

CRANK: Mitchell, how I get to Hunnert Twenny-fifth?

BLOW: One Ten, Crank.

MITCHELL: Go down to T-Square take the crosstown shuttle to Grand Central. Take the I R T uptown express to Eighty-sixth. Take the uptown local get off One Ten. *(Pause)*

CRANK: I come in from Brooklyn I R T.

MITCHELL: That's the *Seventh* Avenue I R T. You want the *Lex* I R T.

BLOW: Fuck, take the E or the A up Eighth Avenue.

MITCHELL: What the fuck he do that? He can't transfer uptown offa the I N D.

BLOW: So fuck it he go to Queens Plaza. There's two shuttles he prob'ly end up Queens anyhow.

CRANK: Oh fuck I don't wanna go to Queens, Mitchell.

MITCHELL: Take the crosstown, Crank, it stops at Grand Central. Blow's right. You take the Queensborough you end up Kew Gardens, Jamaica—some fuckin' place.

CRANK: Jesus I hope them niggers is down on Forty-deuce. How many fuckin' shuttles I have to ride?

MITCHELL: There's only one shuttle. Queensborough acts like a shuttle only she's not.

BLOW: Or hey. Take the N train or the Double R uptown at Forty-ninth. You get off at Fifty-ninth transfer to the Lex no problem.

MITCHELL: Look. The B M T goes out to Queens we got the same problem.

CRANK: Blow, I don't wanna go to Queens.

MITCHELL: Take the crosstown shuttle not the Queensborough and it fuckin' dies at Grand Central. End of the line. You can sit there all fuckin' day it will never go to Queens.

CRANK: I know how to take the B-way local. What happens I take that?

MITCHELL: You end up in the Bronx after about two weeks.

BLOW: Crank, come on. We go down to T-Square I got to connect. Prob'ly the dyke is in that bar?

MITCHELL: Well, you *could* take the B-way local uptown to Two Hunnert Fifteen. Then take the *downtown* to Hunnert and Ten and Lenox and walk over. Or hey—

(Bathroom door opens and RICKY *steps out.)*

RICKY: *Shit on the cocksuckin' subway, take a fuckin' bus! (Pause)* Up the rectum—I got dizzy queens up the rectum. Blow. Crank. Get your asses *on* the street! *On* the street!

BLOW: Don't push me Ricky—I ram your balls up your nose? *(Pause)*

RICKY: You wanna handle this, bohunk? You handle this you end up two broken knees back on Tomkins Square. Old bohunk ladies grind out cigarettes in your face.

BLOW: So? I go to Brooklyn your wop mother she suck my cock.
(Pause. They are nose to nose.)

RICKY: One halfa Tomkins Square is niggers. The other half is bohunks. The city oughta bomb it.

BLOW: All them greasy wops in Brooklyn how come it don't slide inna ocean?

RICKY: You got a hour, Blow.

BLOW: You make me laugh, Ricky. This all crazy—the niggers and the kid. Get ahold of Roper. Cram the deal. Go downtown.

RICKY: All my life somebody tryin' to keep me from getting mine.

MITCHELL: Jesus Ricky so what are you? Seventeen?

RICKY: *ALL MY FUCKIN' LIFE!*

(There is a long silence, as BLOW *and* RICKY *stare at each other.)*

CRANK: *(To* MITCHELL*)* Anyhow I don't fuckin' hafta go uptown?

MITCHELL: *(Looking at* RICKY*)* You'd of gone the fuck to Queens.

CRANK: *(To* MITCHELL*)* I never was in Queens. This john once he wanted me to go out there his place. In his car? Said he woulda take me this Chinese restaurant. Can you feature me some Chinese restaurant in Queens? With

this old john and the forksticks and eggrolls and shit? *(Pause)* Ricky?
Out to fuckin' Queens?

*(*RICKY *turns abruptly from* BLOW *and stalks into bathroom, slamming the door behind him.* BLOW *crosses slowly to bed, staring at the body. He turns and sinks onto the bed's margin.)*

(Silence)

(Lights out)

ACT TWO

Scene One

(Night)

(JOHN ANTHONY's twisted form, beneath the sheet, is vivid on the bed in the darkened room.)

(RICKY is sitting in a chair stage right of the bed, staring at the body.)

RICKY: *(To the body)* I know I first see you you was gonna bust my balls. You gonna take me with you? Hey. You fetus?

(There is a knocking at the door.)

RICKY: Night before last you was upstate prob'ly some treehouse playin' all the other kids. Lakes and rivers and woods and shit, all that like the Catskills. I was the Catskills once.

(There is a louder knocking.)

RICKY: It's funny, New York. Some kids cute like you they come Manhattan make three, four bills a week. Happens. But you come here you fuckin' cack first time you suck a needle.

(There is a rattling of the door.)

RICKY: Now I'm tellin' you you gotta come through for me. You come here to get your own and you fuck up. So now you get me mine.

(Pounding at door. BLOW's voice. "Ricky!" RICKY rises, goes to door. Admits BLOW. RICKY returns to chair by bed, glumly staring at body as before. BLOW closes door, hesitates, then moves to bed, on the margin of which he sits, facing RICKY. BLOW throws a lid of grass on RICKY's lap.)

BLOW: She smoke enough a that you can show movies between her tits.

(RICKY does not respond; he continues to stare at the body throughout most of the remaining dialogue.)

BLOW: Hey. I brung it like you ask?

RICKY: So O K. So now what you fuck? Go down the Haymarket hang out Crank and Mitchell. They come back when the niggers get here.

BLOW: I hang out right here.

RICKY: You fuck you hang out here.

BLOW: You gonna handle Roper?

RICKY: I handle everything. I don't want you here Roper come, Blow.

BLOW: It don't take long Roper know the kid is cacked.

RICKY: He stoned so bad who knows? I figure five, ten minutes he get into somethin'—it don't matter what.

BLOW: You better make it five minutes, Ricky.

RICKY: Just to be alone this room with the fetus, that's all it takes.

BLOW: Maybe even two minutes, Ricky.

RICKY: He don't have to think he kill the kid's ass you know with his own fuckin' hands. Just you know to *be* here. Then I come back he got to buy his way out. This one will handle Roper, Blow.

BLOW: So how much you tell him to bring? You promise the niggers five G's.

RICKY: You don't tell a guy like Roper how much. You just say I got this specialty piece of very young chicken anyway got to bring a wad of C notes. That's all the nigger needs to see. It don't matter Roper got the card. *(Pause)*

BLOW: The card?

RICKY: The card you know you go to this bank day or night shove it in money comes out. You know them automatic machines, bills come shootin' out.

BLOW: What, you march him down to some machine?

RICKY: Everything is by machine. You put your card inna slot. The bank door opens. We go in. He put the card this one machine it tell him how much he got. I want five G's to start the job. He go to this other machine he tell it how much we need. Hey. Machine. Get your fuckin' ass in gear I want five round ones. Machine go, sure, why the fuck not? All these bills pop out.

BLOW: What you, march him down to some machine he dusted to the tits? *(Pause)*

RICKY: So anyway he got to bring a buncha C's that keep the nigger happy til I use the fuckin' card. I don't want you here Roper come, Blow.

BLOW: You just gonna have him see the kid like this?

RICKY: So?

(BLOW *stands by bed and very tenderly arranges the boy's body beneath the sheet so that it appears to be sleeping, the head partially exposed and nestled into a pillow.*)

BLOW: He shouldn't *look* like a dead body.

RICKY: Some off the roof got some weird for this dead fuckin' fetus.

BLOW: *(Sitting on bed again.)* I help you get Roper dusted he get here. You need me, Ricky.

RICKY: My asshole.

BLOW: You need me for Roper. I *do* Roper. I *know* Roper.

RICKY: *(Looking at* BLOW *for the first time.)* What you want from me, Blow?

BLOW: You let me set him up, Ricky, so he don't find out the kid is dead.

RICKY: You gonna mess me, Blow, this crazy shit with the fetus?

BLOW: Crazy so what?

RICKY: I handle it, Blow.

BLOW: She laugh at you, Ricky. Your deal go down the toilet.

RICKY: I was a player, Blow, East New York. This girl was so hot for me—

BLOW: Shit, Ricky. *(Pause)*

RICKY: So O K. O K, *bohunk.* I'm gonna let you stay. I'm gonna let you stay know why?

BLOW: Why, Ricky?

RICKY: So you can face it, Blow. So you can face I am runnin' this deal.

(Pause)

BLOW: Sure, Ricky.

*(*RICKY *throws lid at* BLOW.*)*

RICKY: Now roll a couple.

BLOW: Yeah, O K, Ricky. *(He begins rolling joints.)*

RICKY: So lissen to me, Blow. We got to hot Roper up.

BLOW: Who the fuck you talkin' to, Ricky?

RICKY: We got to get him so hot he don't look at the kid so close 'til we leave. So hot maybe he give head to one of us.

BLOW: Ditn't I tell you Roper bounce off the wall, Ricky?

RICKY: He won't be so cocksuckin' smooth he get fucked up.

BLOW: You handle this dust, Ricky?

RICKY: I got a choice?

BLOW: This stuff black and white you know what I mean? It hits you like speed. Everything goes black, except for the lights, and they like go white.

RICKY: Shitface.

BLOW: Roper gets most of it anyway. You toke, he toke. I toke, he toke. You toke, he toke. Know what I mean?

(There is a knocking at the door, three evenly spaced thumps.)

RICKY: *(Standing)* The john.

(RICKY goes to door. Admits ROPER, who is carrying a briefcase. RICKY leads ROPER back to the bed.)

RICKY: Hey. Mr Roper. Have a seat.

(ROPER remains standing, peering around the room. Sets down briefcase.)

ROPER: Why is it so dark in here?

RICKY: We was getting' stoned. You member Blow?

BLOW: Hey, Mr Roper.

ROPER: Of course. How are you, Blow? We had a session, when was it? Several months ago. Why is it so dark in here?

RICKY: We was getting' stoned, the kid got wrecked. Fuckin' out of it. Have a seat, Mr Roper?

(ROPER remains standing. He eyes JOHN ANTHONY's body.)

ROPER: How wrecked is "wrecked"?

RICKY: Fuck you know he's just in from upstate. What a twelve-year-old kid know from good dope in fuckin' Utica?

ROPER: Looks like a nice kid.

BLOW: A sweetheart, Mr Roper.

ROPER: Have you fucked him, Blow?

RICKY: Hey. Mr Roper. I tell you the kid is fresh. Nobody lay his dirty fingers—

ROPER: Yes, of course, Ricky. *(He seats himself next to bed, in chair previously occupied by RICKY.)* So tell me, Blow, how is it going? I've often wondered what became of you.

BLOW: I'm O K, Mr Roper. But I'm gonna be better after this joint. It's the horniest fuckin' grass I ever smoke.

ROPER: Really? The boy doesn't seem at all excited.

RICKY: He been smokin all day waitin' for you. I hadda give him somethin' to do so I feed him this shit like it was pretzels?

ROPER: How horny, Blow, did the kid get?

BLOW: I don't know I'm in and out.

RICKY: Hot as a firecracker, Mr Roper. Lay there strokin' himself. Now he's like fuckin' putty.

ROPER: Yeah? Well, I'd like to take a look in a moment, if it's all right with you, Blow.

RICKY: What the fuck with Blow?

ROPER: Well, I assume it's Blow who broke him in. It usually is you, isn't it, Blow?

RICKY: Ditn't I tell you? The kid's fresh.

BLOW: Ricky's right, Mr Roper. *(He lights a joint.)* Have a toke, Mr Roper?

(ROPER accepts the joint.)

ROPER: Why not, if it's as good as you say?

RICKY: Mr Roper. I would lie to you? You a businessman. This one a businessman. Satisfaction guaranteed.

ROPER: *(Toking between sentences.)* A businessman, Ricky, is one who has a product to sell or a product to buy. A consultant, who is not a businessman, places the two in relation. I am a consultant. I dislike, I even a little resent, being made to barter like a Puerto Rican shill. For some discount shop. On Fourteenth Street. *You* understand me, don't you, Blow?

RICKY: What the fuck with Blow?

ROPER: I can't imagine *what*, the other week, you were doing in front of Exxon, Blow. You couldn't have been more conspicuously out of place. *(He remembers the joint in his fingers.)* Oh. *(Hands joint to* RICKY. *To* BLOW*)* Did you suppose I'd think you cute for leering at me?

(RICKY tokes quickly and hands joint back to ROPER.*)*

RICKY: Blow is very uncool sometimes, Mr Roper. Me, I am always cool.

BLOW: Hey. Mr Roper. You was alone, wadn't you?

ROPER: *(Toking)* I am never alone on Sixth Avenue, Blow. *(He hands joint to* BLOW *who tokes and hands it back.)*

RICKY: Hey. Mr Roper. You don't have to worry, this kid is top quality product.

ROPER: Top quality product. Indeed. *(Toking)* Augie should be in on this conversation. He likes talking "product." I indulge him of course. Do you know why, Blow?

BLOW: No, Mr Roper. Why?

ROPER: Well, sometimes I think that treating you kids as "product" is our way of keeping you at arm's length. On Sixth Avenue, it's one thing, don't you see? One is indifferent to particulars. But on Eighth Avenue we cannot really, I mean not really, be free from particular sorts of sensations involving particular sorts of boys. Hence the vocabulary of commodities. A distancing device. *(He remembers the joint in his fingers.)* Oh. *(He tokes and hands joint to* RICKY. *He is mechanically echoing the same action he performed earlier.)* I keep forgetting you're there, Ricky.

*(*RICKY *tokes hastily and at once hands joint back to* ROPER.*)*

RICKY: That's O K, Mr Roper.

ROPER: You're not terribly appreciative of this dope, are you, Ricky?

RICKY: Just like the kid I smoke it all day. *(Gestures towards* JOHN ANTHONY*)* Take a look. Blow, get up so's he can take a look.

ROPER: In a moment, Blow. *(He tokes and passes joint to* BLOW.*)* The word is "product", kids. We can't after all admit to being in your power. It was the feeling of being without power that made me hurt you, Blow.

BLOW: *(Toking; coldly)* You ditn't hurt me, Mr Roper.

ROPER: Didn't I? You seemed so—well, so upset at the time.

*(*BLOW *passes joint to* ROPER.*)*

BLOW: Part of the fuckin' scene, man.

ROPER: What? Oh, I think I see. You acted upset because I *wanted* you to act upset. *(Toking)* Or rather, you *thought* I *wanted* you to act upset.

BLOW: Hey, Mr Roper. You get off?

ROPER: By which you mean, don't you, that so long as I derive pleasure from your reaction it doesn't matter what I want your reaction to be? In short, you modulate my desires?

BLOW: Hey. Mr Roper. What you want from me?

ROPER: You see, Blow, that's exactly what I'm talking about. I derive the most intense pleasure from knowing that your body is being purchased in the same way as toothpaste or a pair of shoes. It's tit for tat, kids. Our tyranny as opposed to yours. *(He remembers the joint in his fingers.)* Oh. *(Mechanically again, a bit too mechanically, he tokes and passes joint to* RICKY, *whom he does not look at.)* Your fucking stomach, Blow.

BLOW: Hey. What's the point, Mr Roper?

*(*RICKY *tokes quickly and holds joint towards* ROPER, *who does not notice.)*

ROPER: Your slightly swollen belly. It was hard, it was muscular, but it was also a trifle bloated. In a very sexy way. *(Pause)*

BLOW: Hey, forget it, Mr Roper.

ROPER: It was asking to be ravaged. White and firm as a mound of butter. And then the streak of blood. *(Pause)*

RICKY: *(Looking at* BLOW*)* Jesus. *(He forgetfully raises joint to his lips, tokes, remembers, and nervously extends it towards* ROPER *again.)* Mr Roper.

ROPER: *(Taking joint)* I couldn't show up at the office for a week. *(Toking)* Blow, always direct your fists at a man's body, where the damage won't be noticeable. *(Passes joint to* BLOW*)*

BLOW: I ditn't hurt your fucking face, Mr Roper. That was all in your head. I just slap you around a little. *(With a pronounced shrug)* Know what I mean? *(He has not toked; passes joint to* ROPER.*)*

ROPER: No, I *don't* know what you mean, Blow. *(He begins aping* BLOW's *shrug, markedly overdoing it.)* How *could* I know? Did you know I spent a week with a certain doctor out on the Island? *(He is shrugging wildly now.)* No, kiddo, I *don't* know what you mean. What *do* you mean, Blow? Are you calling me a liar, Blow? What do you mean, Blow?

RICKY: Whyn't you tell Augie, Mr Roper? Or Mike? They break his fuckin' arm.

*(*ROPER *is suddenly quiet.)*

ROPER: This J has gone out.

RICKY: Wait 'til you see this one, Mr Roper. You think Blow got a stomach—

ROPER: *(To* RICKY*)* I told you this J has gone out.

RICKY: Hey. Blow. A match for Mr Roper.

*(*BLOW *takes joint from* ROPER, *lights it, and hands it back.)*

BLOW: Come on, Mr Roper. This shit I don't feature. You wanna play with razor blades you shoulda let me know before, that's all. But even so what I do? I don't break your face. I break your face like Ricky says you get me killed.

ROPER: *(Toking)* Next time I *will* have you killed.

BLOW: *(Laughing)* Hey, Mr Roper. *(Cups his crotch with hand)* What you want—you wanna suck my cock?

RICKY: Yeah, Mr Roper, don't be shy. Suck his fuckin' cock. We'll have a party.

ROPER: A party, Ricky? No one's going to touch *you.*

(Pause)

RICKY: Hey. Blow. Show Mr Roper the merchandise.

ROPER: *(Toking)* The "merchandise." You're not Jewish, are you, Ricky?

BLOW: Mr Roper, you don't grow up New York?

ROPER: Why do you ask, Blow?

BLOW: Shit, Ricky and me we grow up New York.

ROPER: *(Toking)* And therefore—?

BLOW: *(Shrugging)* You know.

(ROPER begins shrugging grotesquely again.)

ROPER: *What* do I know? Tell me. What?

RICKY: The kid's from upstate, Mr Roper.

BLOW: Mr Roper, you from upstate?

ROPER: Why do you ask, Blow?

BLOW: I don't know, Mr Roper.

ROPER: Why do you ask, Blow? *(Pause. He is shrugging crazily.)* Why do you ask? Why do you ask, Blow?

BLOW: Well, you know, me and Ricky ain't the same as you.

(ROPER is suddenly quiet. Tokes and passes joint to BLOW)

ROPER: I don't understand what you're trying to say. Are you trying to say that growing up in New York makes a person obnoxious? Makes him small and ugly and cheap?

RICKY: Hey. Mr Roper. So what's it like upstate? Like the Catskills, right? My people drive to the Catskills one summer I was a kid.

ROPER: Oh, *that* must have been fun. A trail of beer cans. Pizza rinds. Prosciutto. Wax paper. Olive pits. All the way to Woodstock. *(Pause)*

(BLOW, who hasn't toked, hands joint to ROPER.)

RICKY: You grow up Utica, Mr Roper? The kid's from Utica.

ROPER: I grew up, Ricky, in Connecticut.

BLOW: Hey, Mr Roper. I think you must be horny. You wanna bite cock, Mr Roper? Then somebody rip you back, make you come.

ROPER: I am not horny, Blow, in the least. *(Tokes, looks at joint, and places it in ashtray on the floor.)* This grass is lethal.

(BLOW places another joint in his mouth.)

BLOW: Hey. Let's do another one. Get fucked up.

ROPER: I never abdicate control, Blow, when I'm messing with trade. Part of the attraction is that you're unpredictable.

(BLOW begins pawing himself.)

BLOW: Hey. Mr Roper. I can see you now. Down on your fuckin' knees lickin' my thighs. I say, Hey, Mr Roper, you gettin me wet. You don't slobby my balls my cock. You clean my asshole, maybe. *(Spreading legs)* That's

right, Roper, up my shitty asshole—you can't have my cock you pussy.
(To RICKY*)* Then Roper get mad, you know what I mean?

RICKY: Sure. Roper's no kinna guy licks dirty asshole.

BLOW: *(Lighting joint)* Fuck no. So he start to pinch and slap and grab.
He jab his thumb up my asshole I start to yell.

RICKY: His fuckin' fingernail rippin' your asshole.

BLOW: Rippin' my asshole *inside* my asshole. Cuttin' me inside, man. That's
what hots up Mr Roper. Hey. Mr Roper. *(Deadly)* That's what hots you up.
Inside. *(He passes joint to* ROPER, *who accepts it but does not toke.)*

ROPER: You guys should go on television.

RICKY: The whole thing is inside, that's the whole thing about it.

*(*ROPER, *without toking, extends joint towards* RICKY.*)*

RICKY: *(Quickly)* Hey. No. No thanks, man.

*(*ROPER *extends joint towards* BLOW.*)*

ROPER: Blow?

BLOW: You take it, Mr Roper. Right, that's the whole thing. You can whip
some motherfuck or you can cut him or you can chaindance on his face.
But it's inside, that's where you got to go.

RICKY: That's what we sell, man. We don't sell our outsides what you fuck?

BLOW: Right. Don't sell ass or cock. Sell tickets to our insides. The liver,
all them rubbery round things, your fuckin' spine and shit.

ROPER: *(Toking)* Television. That's exactly the medium.

BLOW: Come on, Ricky.

RICKY: Hey. Mr Roper. You can go through every catalog this town you
won't find pussy this sweet this young this hot.

ROPER: I'm sure I won't, Ricky.

RICKY: Know what the kid tell me today? He say he gonna get so out of
it that what he wants he wants to wake up and see some guy doin' him.
And then you know he can't stop it, just lay there through the whole thing.
Nothin' you can't do to him he fuckin' *wants* you to do shit to him. If he was
just a hooker Mr Roper he give out with limits. But this kid Mr Roper he
wants *you* to find his limits.

BLOW: What's this shit, Ricky? Mr Roper knows what he wants.

ROPER: *(Toking)* His body is too white.

RICKY: So what you want—a nigger?

ROPER: This grass is... *(He throws joint in the ashtray.)*

RICKY: Hey. Mr Roper. *(He crosses to other side of bed, to stand by chair looking at* ROPER.*)* Look. I charge you what you think is fair. You do him a little. You don't like it you come downstairs I'm at the Haymarket.

ROPER: The body is too white. The sheets are too white. The whole thing is sickening.

(Pause while RICKY *and* BLOW *exchange looks.)*

BLOW: Look, Mr Roper. You think now you think it make you throw up. It always comes off like that at first.

RICKY: Sure. But you get into it later.

BLOW: I know you, Mr Roper. You ain't like them other johns. Rubbin' up against me and actin' like a bitch. But you actin like a bitch now, Mr Roper, and that ain't you—you fuckin' get tired with that. You a man, Mr Roper. A man has got to be master. That's why you like guys. Every cocksuck can make a bitch do his shit. But here's this kid. And he sayin' to you, O K man show me some cock. I been dreamin' about this, now you take me down the street you show me some cock.

RICKY: Sure. These little out-of-town numbers the hardest ones. They been savin' it up inside like if you ditn't jack off for twelve years that's what this kid is like. You be sorry you don't try it, Mr Roper.

BLOW: You be sorry later, Mr Roper. You a man, Mr Roper, and you got to show this kid some real fuckin' cock.

RICKY: He never see real fuckin' cock, Mr Roper, not like you gonna show him.

BLOW: No shit cock, Mr Roper.

RICKY: Real motherfuckin' cock, Mr Roper.

ROPER: *(Screaming)* GET OUT! *(Pause. Covers his face with his hands)*

RICKY: Sure, Mr Roper.

BLOW: O K, Mr Roper.

*(*RICKY *and* BLOW *move towards door, pause, look back at* ROPER. BLOW *looks anxiously at bed. The boys exit. After a pause* ROPER *drops his hands and looks about him in the darkness, hugging himself.)*

ROPER: Why is it so dark in here? *(Suddenly, he stands; looks down at* JOHN ANTHONY.*)* That's right. Just lie there. *(Pause. Then he begins to pace to and fro before the bed as he speaks.)* Never overdo the drugs when you're dealing with trade. On the other hand, I feel so stupid if I don't take my share. *(Mumbling)* Why do I sound so pathetic? *(To* JOHN ANTHONY*)* You see yourself how strong this grass is. Dynamite, isn't that the word? Nitroglycerine. I tell myself, you ass, don't keep toking away like a chimney. At first you feel so powerful. Then so afraid. *(Mumbling)* Only one

joint, I'm falling to pieces over one joint? *(He halts abruptly.)* Was it treated
with something? Blow wouldn't dare. I'd have him killed. *(Resumes pacing.
To* JOHN ANTHONY*)* Killed, do you understand? I've been a customer on
these streets for years. This is New York City, kiddo. You put out, you
produce, you deliver. *(Suddenly giggling)* Such a by god movie. Everything
you feel, every thought you express, it's like a pound of pastrami laid on
a deli counter. *(Goofing)* Is it fresh? Of course it's fresh. Would we sell you
meat wasn't one hunnert percent fresh? Listen, we make a *nice* sandwich.
(Mumbling) That wasn't coherent. *(To* JOHN ANTHONY*)* Why do I say things
like, "Part of your attraction, my dear Blow, is that you are unpredictable"?
Did you hear that? No wonder I get laughed at behind my back by these
twats. Behind my back? Blow was laughing at me right to my *face. (Halts)*
He's a good lay, that boy. Isn't he? Well, it's going to be a bit rougher
with me, kiddo. *(Resumes pacing)* Now, poppers, I like poppers. Or coke.
Coke and poppers, they're all body. But grass, I've never gotten used to it,
sometimes it's so totally a matter of the thoughts, the fears, the little
needling doubts. Like acid, like...like all those *mind*-fucking drugs.
Of course, you just let your fears, I suppose the word is, vomit out of you.
Normally I don't carry on like this, this grass is very, as you know
very...That's right. Just lie there. *(Pause as he stares down at* JOHN ANTHONY*)*
I brought some toys, kiddo. I may just handcuff you to the bed. *(He goes to
briefcase, opens it, pauses.)* Only I don't believe I'm going to fuck you after all.
Too bad. *(Pauses. Resumes pacing)* You're lying there expecting me to tear
into you, aren't you? You think by playing dead animal I'll really make a
mess of you, don't you? Well, think again, kiddo. You don't excite me at all.
You disgust me. *(Halts; looks about him)* God, it's dark in here. *(Resumes
pacing)* Actually I rather enjoy these sleazy pits. Not for the cliché reasons,
I assure you. Not because I have a hard-on for filth, not because I'm
slumming, like some oleomargarine leather queen. *(Mumbling)* Am I even
in the slightest degree coherent? *(Abruptly laughing)* I like the drama of it,
goddamn it. I *like* sitting here with these cheap little tarts and putting on a
show! I *like* playing roles. Oh, you'll learn about playing parts if you stick
around New York City, kiddo! Sometimes, with a client, I'll give him a taste
of something besides the "exquisite bland". I did *not* come off the parking
lot and rise to be president of the corporation. *Not* some glossy puppet,
acquiring all those funny mannerisms such a creature thinks is required. I'm
an independent, essentially. I have the correct background, and I'm told it
shows. I am *not* smooth. Effortless. There's a subtle difference. Impeccably
businesslike, don't you know, but effortless. My mind is really—it literally
glares at them!—engaged with them only at the most superficial level.
(Halts. Resumes pacing) No, the structure of, what shall I call it? Painful
intimacy. Intimacy always is painful. It has taken me years to discover
that. Getting painfully close to someone in this town is a bit unsubtle? Yes,
decidedly unsubtle for my taste. *(Halts. Hugs himself.)* Cold in here. Middle
of August and I'm cold. Those sheets, I'm sure those sheets haven't been

washed in months. Yet they're blinding me. Like your body. The sun comes
out, suddenly everything aches, everything is colder. Very disagreeable.
(Pause) Snow...I'm talking about snow. *(Resumes pacing. Mumbling)*
Something's wrong. *(To* JOHN ANTHONY*)* I don't usually carry on like this.
Some grass, hey kiddo? *(Pause)* That's right. Just lie there. Nothing, kiddo,
is more boring than pointless motion! *(Resumes pacing)* I would describe
Blow as plump, wouldn't you? Rosy, plump and frozen solid. Rather like a
perfect small fowl you might pick up at the supermarket. Naturally I don't
mean to make you jealous. There is a clientele for your sort, believe me.
And this silent fuck-me routine is even more seductive. What's this?
(Discovers T-shirt among sheets) Is this part of your drag, honey? The Big
Apple? It's actually a big banana, Mary, and they'll ram it right up your
uterus. *(Mumbling)* Who said that? Who in hell delivered *that* line? *(To* JOHN
ANTHONY.*)* Put it on. *(Throws T-shirt at body.)* Put it on. I want you naked
from the waist down. *(Pause)* Put it on. *(Pause)* I told you to put it on. *(Pause)*
Put it on! *(Clutches T-shirt, slaps body with it.)* Put it on put it on put it on!
Know what I mean? *(He begins wildly shrugging again.)* Know what I mean?
Do you? Hey, man, youse know what I fuckin' mean?

(Throws T-shirt at body. Abruptly begins pacing again.)

ROPER: Passion in grown men—don't you think?—is never quite real.
Passion, the real stinking hots, spring from the child in us. You kids are
very close to that. But there must be something fierce and dominant, too.
Something I can provoke, and then break. That's where you lose, kiddo.
Now, Blow...now Blow understands. *(Halts.)* Blow might have done very
well, if he'd had half a chance. Had the right clothes, the right background,
the right tone. *(Abruptly, he sits in chair by bed. Shakily lights a cigarette)*
The world I move in, well, it's a tad abstract. Everything changes
hands—money, whole corporations, people's careers and yet there's
only the sound of paper rasping against fingertips. Only the vaguest of
connections, you know. But you kids...you're such wonderfully foul little
creatures. So very *alive.* In my world, kiddo, I sometimes think the fellows
themselves were spawned in the bowels of Xerox machines. Still there is a
kind of grace, an unconscious flowing ease, among those who gain control
over others. To see it, kiddo, is as important as having it. When I encounter
it—as I did the other day, a lawyer, in admiralty, patents, bankruptcy,
anyhow some really shabby corner of the legal profession. This fellow had it
all. Moved like a dream. Yet an abrupt boyishness. His grin was positively
sardonic. *(Pause)* Does he go home on the 6:15 and dandle little waxen
creatures on his knee? The wife, oh yes, there's a wife in there somewhere.
Petite, blonde, skinny, wonderfully blank expression. Her voice crackles
like potato chips. Kelly green lawns, the fine spray of sprinklers, a tricycle
overturned, a Chris Craft in the driveway. I'm not, kiddo, putting it down.
Not one of your sour city queens. There must be these differences, these
several motivations. He plays the game for the good of his little family; it's a

hallowed tradition, and I don't dispute it. It's simply that there are, don't you know, higher motivations. Finer vibrations. For the family man, you see, it's the money he's after, the security. He doesn't see the process for the forest of bucks. And the process, kiddo, is the most beautiful thing in the world. *(He stands up abruptly and begins pacing again.)* It can take greed, lust, fraud, every conceivable vileness, and produce not only the wealth, not only the action and purpose and point, but all the amenity, all the grace, all the complication that makes for interest, that makes for life. You learn to refine as it refines. You learn to see past the throngs of little hustlers with their warts and styes and meanness, their tiny bunkered deals. They're simply the what-do-you-call-'em? The ratchets and sprockets of an immense process that knows what it wants, that dices and selects and arranges according to its own lights. People keep looking for gods to worship. But they're already living in God's belly! When once you see it, it's exhilarating. Through all this there is this grace. Now that lawyer—*he* was capable of seeing it. But he fell for babies made of styrofoam and pineapple sundae wives. He fell short of the vision. *(Halts)* That's what one wants, kiddo. Someone at one's own level. Someone who understands. *(He sits in chair again.)* There *is* this grace. *(He leans forward, hugging himself.)* I swear there's an icicle down my spine. *(Rises and begins pacing again)* You saw of course what Blow was doing? That cheap device of digging at one's masculinity— in his hands it really amounts to a kind of satanism. The little twat. *(Begins twitching)* I took away *his* phony manhood the last time. Just reached up and—slit!—he had his first period! He brings it out of me. He's some kind of devil, some kind of filthy little devil. Popped his cherry, though, popped it good. God, the color of blood on that swelling skin. For a moment he just looked at me, big startled eyes. He was a little boy all of a sudden, it was as if I'd maimed a child. I wanted.... *(Halts, shivering)* I wanted to take him in my arms. I wanted to comfort him. *(Pacing again)* That's how we have it. Blow understands that. The kid screams. You gather him in your arms. That's how we have it. Like I say—he'd have made fine management. *(Pause)* But Blow is a twat. Oh, he knows how we have it. It's not that he hasn't played the battered boy for a thousand clients. But he wants to direct the show. The clients don't know it, maybe, but *he* has to be in charge. *(To* JOHN ANTHONY.*)* Well, nobody's in charge of *me*, kiddo. *(Halts. Shivers violently. Stares at* JOHN ANTHONY*)* I'm so cold.... Please... Don't think badly of me... *(He climbs into bed; huddles under sheet, nestling against* JOHN ANTHONY's *body.)* That's right. Just lie there.

(Silence)

(Lights down)

Scene Two

(The same, a few moments later. Lights rise once again to glow on the bed, on the entwined forms beneath the sheet. There is the rasp of the automatic lock, and RICKY and BLOW enter tentatively through entrance door.)

RICKY: Hey. Mr Roper? *(Pause)* I forgot somethin', Mr Roper. In the bat'room? *(He approaches bed.)* Will you fuckin' look at this?

BLOW: I don't have to look.

RICKY: Hey. Mr Roper.

(He shakes ROPER's body.)

RICKY: He's out of it.

BLOW: You smoke that shit like he did you be out of it too.

(RICKY lifts the sheet, then drops it.)

RICKY: Like a coupla babies.

(BLOW moves downstage to inspect the opened briefcase.)

BLOW: He hardly even touch the toys. All this shit packed in here like his mother was sendin' him to summer camp.

RICKY: I figure he have the kid hangin' by his balls.

BLOW: Roper?—Shit.

RICKY: How you know that?

BLOW: I know Roper.

RICKY: Blow, he fuckin' cut you.

BLOW: Shit. You know what it was like? She was lickin' my balls and then it was like she goes— *(Gestures limply)* "Take that, Mary." Like with this blade she had hid in her fist. She just scratch me so I would beat the fuck outa her.

RICKY: You crazy, Blow.

(RICKY stares at BLOW, then abruptly begins shaking ROPER.)

RICKY: Hey. Roper. Jesus. Mr Roper. Hey. The kid, Mr Roper. What the fuck did you do? *(Pause)* Hey. Fuck. The kid is dead!

BLOW: She's gone uptown, Ricky. She gonna be there awhile. I got the shakes I don't even smoke half.

RICKY: I don't smoke it anyhow I'm fucked up from last night.

BLOW: You leave my dope in the bat'room?

RICKY: My fit. Your dope. How long before she come around? *(He sits in chair by the bed.)* I give her a few minutes. You get weird maybe but you don't get wrecked like this.

BLOW: That was strong shit, Ricky.

(Again RICKY *stares at* BLOW. *Then he leans forward, addressing* ROPER.*)*

RICKY: The kid is dead, Mr Roper. What we gonna do? Hey, Mr Roper. What the fuck we gonna do?

BLOW: Would you fuck off with that shit?

RICKY: *(To* BLOW*)* You do deliveries for me? Upper East? I can't send Crank Upper East.

BLOW: You don't got it yet, Ricky.

RICKY: It's in the pocket. *(He rises, bends over bed and rummages under the sheet; withdraws* ROPER's *wallet. Looks through it)* What's *this* bullshit. There's what there's maybe what? A halfa fuckin' C in her purse! What she think I gonna *bill* her?

BLOW: Mike prob'ly does.

*(*RICKY *begins violently shaking and slapping* ROPER.*)*

RICKY: Hey. You bitch. Get the fuck up! The kid is dead you bitch! I gotta get her outa here, now you get up!

*(*ROPER *stiffens under the blows, eyes open wildly.)*

ROPER: Please.

RICKY: You fuckin' asshole you get me in a shitty mess! You get me in a shitty mess you fuckin' asshole!

ROPER: Please.

RICKY: This ain't gonna be cheap, you cocksuck you pussy!

ROPER: *(Screaming)* Please! *(He curls into a tight ball and buries his head in the pillows.)*

*(*RICKY *drops into chair.)*

RICKY: I give her a few minutes. We take the card, we go downstairs.

BLOW: How you gonna get her down to talk to some machine? She screamin' and shakin, and you say—Hey. Machine. My friend she's out of it but anyway you bitch put out. Hey. You bitch. Put the fuck out. Who crazy, Ricky? *You* crazy, Ricky.

RICKY: Shut your fuck, Blow. *(Pause)*

BLOW: Niggers be here wantin' fat five, and you ain't even got one.

RICKY: Shut your fuck, Blow. *(Pause)* Why you get it so strong? *(Pause)* Blow? What else you got in there?

BLOW: Dust, man. Dust.

RICKY: Dust don't turn you no babyshit.

BLOW: Some people disco on this shit.

RICKY: What else you got in there, bohunk!

(When BLOW *does not respond,* RICKY *abruptly rises and attacks* ROPER *again.)*

RICKY: You pussy I gotta have five G's I gotta have five G's you pussy!

(He tries to pull ROPER *from bed.)*

*(*ROPER, *his eyes shut, rolls over and grasps* JOHN ANTHONY's *body.)*

RICKY: Get your pussy up you fuck!

BLOW: Stop that shit, Ricky.

RICKY: *(Still pulling at* ROPER*)* Five G's five G's five G's.

*(*BLOW *crosses to bed and shoves* RICKY *aside, then begins struggling with* ROPER.*)*

BLOW: Get your fuckin' hands *offa* him, Roper!

(He disengages ROPER *from* JOHN ANTHONY.*)*

ROPER: *(Screaming)* Please!

BLOW: You don't touch that kid you hear me, Roper?

(He pulls ROPER *from the bed onto the floor.)*

*(*ROPER *in panic scrambles under bed.)*

RICKY: *(To* BLOW*)* So what you fuck? Now how I get him outa there?

BLOW: He don't touch the kid, that's all.

RICKY: The kid is dead, asshole!

BLOW: He don't touch him, that's all.

*(*RICKY *drops on his knees to shout under bed.)*

RICKY: Get outa there you pussy! Oh Jesus.

BLOW: That nigger cut you good, Ricky, you don't got somethin to show him.

*(*RICKY *manages to drag* ROPER *from beneath bed.* ROPER *is wound in a tight ball, fists crossed over chest, chin pressed into arms, eyes closed.)*

RICKY: *(Placating.)* Roper. Listen. I gotta go down to the bank. What's the code number for this fuckin' card?

*(*ROPER *does not respond.)*

RICKY: The code number. Mr Roper. Hey. The number.

(ROPER *wriggles back under the bed.*)

RICKY: Oh Jesus.

BLOW: Code number?

RICKY: Gotta have the code you punch in the number.

BLOW: What the fuck, you need a number? She can't tell you her address, and you got to have a number?

(RICKY *stands; abruptly sits in chair.*)

RICKY: I give her a few minutes she come around.

(BLOW *crosses to other side of bed; begins to arrange pillow and sheet around* JOHN ANTHONY's *body.*)

BLOW: You got the niggers a little while, you got Augie at midnight. You ain't got but a coupla bucks. You ain't got the blow. If the nigger leave you on your feet—maybe he's in a hurry? Hey. Maybe he's in a hurry?—if he leave you standin' up then you tell Augie to take it out in trade. Take you maybe—let's see you gonna be maybe sixty when you pay him off. He'll wait. Hey? Then he goes and tells Mike.

RICKY: I give her a few minutes.

BLOW: Give her a few, that's right, Ricky, give her 'til you layin' on the floor holding your guts. I seen it once, a manager he thinks he own the fuckin' bar. They tell him—Hey. You don't own fuckin' nothin'. He deal like he own his own mother ass and they get pissed off. One morning I'm with the bartender he take me into the bar to suck me a quick one you know what I mean? For him it's free. You shoulda seen it, Ricky. *(Pause)* The manager like his head was blown clean fuckin' away. *(Pause)* But it was the manager's punk, some kid he pick up in Florida? *(Pause)* They cut him from his tits to his cock hang him up behind the bar. *(Pause)* So maybe the nigger *don't* cut you. He's a mean cocksucker but he don't kill your ass. Anyway let's don't worry about niggers. It's Mike, man. He think you only lookin' funny at him he tear off your suckin' nose. You and Crank and Mitchell you work outa here like you belong to Mike. Mike think you belong to him he get right away suspicious, think you onna grab. He don't really care what you grab he don't care how much. It's because you reachin' for it. It's when you spread your fingers and lean over—*that's* what give Mike the hots. Just that you want. He hates it that you fuckin' want. *(Pause)* It's like his own face is starin' back at him. *(Pause)*

RICKY: It ain't only my ass, bohunk.

BLOW: Is this one reachin', Ricky? Or Augie, you think Augie is reachin'? Augie's a manager. Managers—it's part of the set-up they get a little. Rip time is part of the set-up. Augie's not reachin'—Mike is *givin'* it to him.

RICKY: I wait a few minutes. You shut your fuck, do what I say.

BLOW: You member that little redhead, the hooker hadda cock bigger than he was? Starts at the Haymarket just like you and me. Member him? He start punkin' for some competitor Mike don't fuckin' like. Big fat pig inna limo drives up to G G's like it was his? So Mike ask the redhead a favor. The redhead he spills to the fat pig in the limo. O K. The fat pig he still drivin' up to G G's like there was searchlights at the door. But the kid they fuckin' peel off his lips. They don't kill his ass but you try suckin' cock when you got no lips on your fuckin' face.

RICKY: The niggers kill my ass. Mike kill my ass. So I fuckin' give her a few minutes, Blow. You hear me, Blow? (*Pause. Then he descends to his knees to shout under bed.*) You fuckin' pussy! You actin' like a bitch you pussy like a little bitch!

BLOW: That won't work with him, Ricky.

RICKY: Oh Jesus.

BLOW: It was crazy from the start, Ricky. Roper you suckin' right, Roper *is* pussy. He don't *like* pussy.

RICKY: Oh Jesus.

BLOW: Roper carry these toys like they was his basket. He come here so maybe the *kid* is gonna show cock. But he can't *act* like pussy. He can't act like pussy Eighth Avenue, he can't act like pussy Sixth. He hopin' the kid will go, Hey. You know with the poppers and shit. Hey. You like it up the ass hey baby hey baby. Roper go, Shut up, kid, real rough like voice down to here. Shut up, kid. Roper is big, but the kid with his pretty face it's the pretty face Roper wants to see over him, bangin' him slappin' him cuttin' him. The kid goes, Hey cunt. Real high, little boy voice. He turns Roper's arm a little, turns his arm a little in the socket. Roper goes, Oh shit, that's my bad arm, kid. Kid goes, Cunt. Cunt. Pussy cunt. Oh baby you pussy cunt feel it up your hole. And there's this pretty little kid wailin' on Roper's ass.

(*There is a knocking at the door.*)

BLOW: The niggers.

(RICKY *rises to his feet, backs towards bathroom door.*)

RICKY: I gotta think, Blow. Lean on 'em a little I gotta....

BLOW: Oh shit, Ricky.

RICKY: They're early. Give 'em the money in her purse. Tell 'em to come back maybe an hour.

BLOW: Oh shit, Ricky.

RICKY: Shut your fuck do what I say, Blow! *(He exits into bathroom, closing door.)*

(BLOW stands in silence, staring after RICKY. There is more knocking, only BLOW does not move. There is knocking again. BLOW abruptly crosses to bed and fusses with sheet, musingly fingering a lock of JOHN ANTHONY's hair.)

(There is more knocking. Finally, BLOW moves upstage to door. Breathes deeply. Whips open door. Enter CRANK and MITCHELL, tentatively, speaking in a kind of hush.)

MITCHELL: What the ka-fuck? You don't let shiksas like us stand around in hallways. Bad enough the street door is broke.

CRANK: Where's Ricky?

(BLOW, relieved, gestures towards bathroom; moves downstage to sit in chair by the bed. He looks into ROPER's wallet, which RICKY has left on the floor next to the chair. CRANK and MITCHELL come tentatively downstage.)

CRANK: *(Continued, in low tones to BLOW)* Thinkin' again?

MITCHELL: So where's all the whips and chains?

(CRANK sits on the bed's right margin.)

CRANK: Is the shit come? Niggers get here yet?

MITCHELL: The halters, you know? The fist scene? Did she even *notice* the kid is cacked?

CRANK: Ricky he got the money. Right, Blow?

MITCHELL: The *kid* is still here. No shit stains on the *ceiling*. What I wanna know is what happened with Roper?

CRANK: Ricky shoult'na had me promise them niggers fat five. Blow? Shoult'na promise.

MITCHELL: It hadda be such a comedy? Up the pee-hole. *(Goofing)* What you mean I kill this kid? All I did was pull her teeth with my silver wrenches.

BLOW: Roper's under the bed.

(CRANK jumps up from bed.)

CRANK: Motherfuck!

MITCHELL: Blow, you shittin' me? *(He descends to knees; peers under bed.)* Hey. You musta fed her enough dust to fill a pothole. She's under there shakin' like a Pekinese. Hey. Mr Roper. Don't worry. It's just you know like it's just temporary. I know it *feels* like permanent brain damage. But tomorrow you get up, you walk around, you take a shit, you get bored, you toke up another, you do it all over again only this time it's a kick in the tits. Laugh?

You will piss your panties, Mr Roper. (*To* BLOW) You get any money offa the bitch?

BLOW: A coupla bucks maybe.

CRANK: A coupla bucks! Hey. Blow. Them niggers is comin' here.

BLOW: And this card you know how to use this card?

MITCHELL: Oh sure niggers take credit cards.

CRANK: So Ricky he's thinkin'? A new operation?

BLOW: Upper East. He work outa one of them services, you know what I mean? Dinners at a French restaurant hunnert dollars a night. Gonna be a *escort.*

MITCHELL: Gonna be a dead man that shvartzer find him.

CRANK: Or Mike?

(*Still on his knees,* MITCHELL *begins hissing under the bed.*)

MITCHELL: Hey. Mr Roper. You this consultant, right? So give us the word. A coupla black bitches, kinna mean but anyway they got a sense of humor? And a low-level capo he likes to bend back your fingers. Then there's us hookers. If you was us hookers, what would you do? Know what I mean? Like if you had this one corporation won't deliver because of you know mismanagement? And there's this other corporation wantin' more money than was ever around in the first place? They ain't got much muscle but *much* muscle they don't need. But the real problem is the third corporation. *They* got muscle. If the first corporation don't put out, then the second don't come across, and then you see what I mean? The third corporation says, O K, sluts, fuck for blood.

CRANK: Blow? Mike gonna rub glass in our eyes?

MITCHELL: So Mr Roper what do they pay you for?

BLOW: Crank, all this time you and Ricky act like you live here.

MITCHELL: So consult our asses, you bitch!

BLOW: You come, you go Crank. Don't tie up with nobody. Keep it small. Keep it like if somebody ask you, can you hold this shit while he fucks off uptown, you say, Oh man I'm too stoned, could you get me a cab?

CRANK: So he's gonna rub glass in our eyes? Blow?

BLOW: I don't know, Crank. Maybe not. Maybe he don't care so much.

MITCHELL: You fuckin' G M queen you fuckin' Sixth Avenue rage piece! (*He suddenly stands; crosses to bureau.*) I'm puttin out for these numbers since I'm fifteen years old. (*He starts brushing his hair before bureau mirror.*) Fulla shit, every one. You know how they get to the fiftieth floor? The fiftieth floor is just fifty blow jobs piled on toppa each other! A lotta two-bit Jews and three-piece Goyim. *(Stops brushing hair; into mirror.)* I'm scared, Blow. *(Pause)*

BLOW: So maybe Mike don't find out everything.

MITCHELL: You knew Mike was gonna find out?

BLOW: I don't know nothin.

MITCHELL: Mike gonna find out, why the ka-fuck you hangin' around?

BLOW: For the kid.

(Pause)

MITCHELL: For that stinkin' corpse?

BLOW: He was a nice kid—ditn't do nothin.

MITCHELL: That kid, Blow? That kid come here for cock. I see her stick her arm out. She wadn't dreamin about you. She was hot for cock. Any cock up her ass in her mouth.

BLOW: Shut up, Mitchell.

(MITCHELL begins violently brushing his hair; speaking into mirror.)

MITCHELL: They look at magazines in Utica, Blow. Come here think it's a magazine, big cocks and hairy chests.

BLOW: Shut the fuck up, Mitchell!

CRANK: Ricky. Maybe Ricky has a new operation?

MITCHELL: *(Ceases brushing; looks hard at BLOW)* You shakin' too, Blow. How much of that shit you suck up?

BLOW: Skin like. All over his body is like the skin on your fuckin' behind.

MITCHELL: *(Rolling his eyes to ceiling)* This the weird room. This the number one weird room onna Deuce.

(There is rasping of the lock; enter AUGIE through entrance door.)

AUGIE: Jeez. Where the fuck is Roper you cunts?

MITCHELL: You a little early ain't you early, Augie?

AUGIE: You end up dead I come at midnight, bitch. Where's Roper?

MITCHELL: Under the bed? *(Pause)*

AUGIE: *(Toneless)* Under the fuckin' bed.

MITCHELL: He crawls under the bed what can we do?

AUGIE: *Drag him outa there!*

(Immediately CRANK and MITCHELL work at pulling ROPER from beneath the bed.)

AUGIE: *(To* BLOW.*)* Where's greaseball?

BLOW: Inna toilet. Niggers be here real soon. You wanna see if they take this card?

AUGIE: Fuckin' jeez. Where you get that?

BLOW: In her wallet. Ricky says you can talk to machines with it.

AUGIE: Give me the fuckin' wallet.

*(*BLOW *hands over card and wallet to* AUGIE.*)*

BLOW: We flash that card at them maybe everything happen like Ricky say.

AUGIE: Niggers ain't runnin this deal no more, so fuck off with the cutes, Blow. *(He crosses to bathroom door, loudly.)* Mike wanna know Ricky come and see him.

(The bathroom door opens. Enter RICKY *with a tourniquet around his arm, holding a syringe.)*

AUGIE: What you doin there, greaseball?

RICKY: Just a taste—so what?

AUGIE: A that same shit offa Blow?

RICKY: Just a taste I said! Now what you fuck?

AUGIE: Mike wants you should come and see him, Ricky.

(Pause)

RICKY: *(Gesturing with "fit")* You a pussy wipe, Augie.

AUGIE: You should be sayin' this to me.

RICKY: You pussied out, Augie, you go to Mike!

AUGIE: To me he says this.

RICKY: We coulda got outa here, Augie! This was in the pocket.

AUGIE: Pussy she calls me. That hurts, asshole.

RICKY: *(Straight into* AUGIE's *face.)* Mike is runnin' this deal? He give you better terms?

BLOW: Hey. Mitchell. I am so fuckin' surprised.

MITCHELL: *(While pulling at* ROPER.*)* And we are so fuckin' crippled.

AUGIE: *(Casually looking away from* RICKY; *to the room.)* Mike ain't gonna hurt nobody.

RICKY: *(Toneless)* Ain't gonna hurt nobody.

AUGIE: I ain't hurt so why he hurt you?

RICKY: You fuckin', you fuckin', you fuckin' tell Mike.

AUGIE: No, I ditn't.

(He crosses to MITCHELL *and* CRANK, *who have succeeded in pulling* ROPER *from under bed.* ROPER *is curled in a ball with arms crossed over chest and eyes shut.)*

AUGIE: Hey. Mr Roper. You know me, it's Augie.

ROPER: Augie?

RICKY: So who tell Mike, Augie?

AUGIE: Hey. Mr Roper. Tits up.

RICKY: Who tell Mike I ask you a fuckin' question!

(Pause. AUGIE *looks at* RICKY, *glances here and there about the room, and then settles his gaze on* BLOW.*)*

AUGIE: So who tell Mike, Blow?

*(*BLOW *does not respond.)*

AUGIE: I wonner who rip the panties off this fuckin' operation? I wonner who call and say, Hey. Mike. Some kinna weird up there those stupid fags. Buncha Gucci Dior coke buncha nigger lowlifes messin' your room. I wonner who do that, Blow?

BLOW: *(Rising and turning away)* I don't work for you, Augie.

AUGIE: *(Rising and crossing to* BLOW; *spinning him around)* Oh yeah right. You come you go you suck you fuck. Don't belong to nobody I heard that shit. Now you answer me, Blow.

RICKY: Blow?

AUGIE: Mike lissen to you you bohunk you cocksuck. And I gotta dance up there and go, Oh shit, I am shocked up my clitteris. Then I gotta say I will find out these fags what they fuckin' doin over there. Twice I gotta dance for Mike. Then I gotta say, Fuckin' jeez, there's not only these niggers and this coke there's this dead fetus. And Mike, what you think Mike say, Blow?

*(*BLOW *does not respond. He is trying to look away, but* AUGIE *keeps ducking his face under* BLOW's *fugitive gaze.)*

AUGIE: He go, Oh? *(Pause)* Oh yeah? *(Pause)* Now why you do that, Blow?

*(*BLOW *turns away without responding.)*

RICKY: You fuckin' answer him, bohunk!

BLOW: Ricky try and sell the kid. *(Pause)*

*(*RICKY *crosses to* BLOW *and stares at his back. Then he slowly turns and approaches bed. Looks at body)*

RICKY: You fetus? You feature this? Blow fuck, he fuck my deal for you, you little shit. He fuckin', he fuckin'....

MITCHELL: Jesus, Blow.

(RICKY *turns from bed and crosses to* BLOW *again and stares at his back as before.* RICKY *raises "fit" menacingly, like a shiv, then despairingly drops hand. He turns from* BLOW, *slowly shaking his head, and crosses to bathroom.*)

AUGIE: Mike thinks maybe you should come and see him, Ricky. He knows you was gonna tell him, but he wants to make sure you unnerstan' the procedures. Knows you wadn't gonna finalize without him. Says to tell you, he admires your fuckin' initiative, Ricky.

(RICKY *enters bathroom soundlessly, carefully closing the door behind him.*)

MITCHELL: Ka-fuck.

(AUGIE *crosses to* BLOW.)

AUGIE: So you don't work for me, right, Blow?

(BLOW *is staring at the body; he does not lift his eyes.*)

BLOW: That's right, Augie.

AUGIE: "That's right, Augie." You fucking right I'm right. The one you workin' for now is Mike.

BLOW: I come I go, Augie.

AUGIE: "I come I go, Augie." You fuckin' right. When Mike say come, you come, when he say go, you go. He says to me I gotta keep a eye on you, Blow. He knows it was your dirt cacked the kid, Blow.

BLOW: You tell him that, Augie?

AUGIE: And he wants your twat outa here down the Village, Blow. (*Pause*)

BLOW: I come I go, Augie.

AUGIE: And when you get more dirt to peddle it comes through this operation. Hey? And when you stick your big bohunk cock up somebody's hole we tell you who's hole, how deep and when to fuckin' shoot. Got that, Blow? (*Pause*)

BLOW: (*Almost a whisper*) So fuckin' what?

AUGIE: "So fuckin' what?" So Mike has got control, that's fuckin' what. Control. The one you workin' for now is Mike. (*He crosses to stand over* ROPER.) Hey. Mr Roper. Mike wants I should take you home.

ROPER: Augie?

AUGIE: Hey. You get kinna fucked up? Fuckin' happens, Mr Roper, know what I mean?

ROPER: Augie?

MITCHELL: So what about the niggers?

AUGIE: Cops take care of them.

MITCHELL: The what, Augie?

AUGIE: *(Checking watch)* You tell Mike those black mothers come here at ten, right, Blow? That don't give us much time, bitches.

CRANK: You mean like police and shit?

AUGIE: Niggers are holdin'. They get here about ten minutes after the Midtown Precinct.

MITCHELL: Augie. I am not dressed for the Midtown Precinct.

AUGIE: Mike got control. I gotta say that. Can you see the big write-up inna *Daily News*? "White Kid Cacked by Dope and Niggers." *(Pause)* What I'm sayin' is the niggers take the heat for the fetus.

(Pause, as the others stare)

AUGIE: Fuckin' Christ. I mean, Mike has got his fingers up product. Cops look good. They take pictures. All them bozos out in Queens eat it up.

CRANK: So the niggers is gonna pay? Augie?

AUGIE: Cops eat some of that coke, we stretch the rest. It's under control. Blow, you hang out the Village for a while. *(Looks hard at* BLOW*)* Like Mike wants.

BLOW: *(Dazed; emotionless)* Cops take care of him, Augie. Send his body home.

AUGIE: *(Toneless)* Send his body home.

BLOW: *(Same)* Mike ain't gonna put the kid in the river. Cops send his body home.

AUGIE: Tie a pink ribbon on his weewee send him right home, Blow. Fuckin' jeez. You all hang out the Village. 'Cept Ricky. Hey. Mr Roper. You wanna try standin' up? That's right.

(He helps ROPER *into a chair.)*

CRANK: Augie? He ain't gonna rub glass in our eyes?

*(*AUGIE *glowers at* CRANK.*)*

AUGIE: Shut your cocksuck.

ROPER: He's not really dead, Augie. He's not really, is he?

AUGIE: Of course not, Mr Roper.

ROPER: A large ugly joke.

AUGIE: A bozo scene—it ain't real.

ROPER: Not real. Of course not. Augie?

CRANK: Blow. He don't break our fingers?

AUGIE: Come on, Mr Roper. This your briefcase, right? *(Picks up briefcase after snapping it shut.)* We get a cab, go to your place, you get inna hot tub. Mike he send you his compliments, says he will take care of everything.

(He helps ROPER *towards the entrance door. To the others)*

AUGIE: You queens got maybe twenny minutes. I don't wanna see your assholes these facilities. Tell Ricky I see him the Haymarket. We go see Mike.

(Exits with ROPER *through entrance door)*

CRANK: Mitchell?

MITCHELL: What the fuck I stash in this pit? *(He crosses to bureau, rummages.)*

CRANK: Mitchell? Our foots ain't gonna be in Brooklyn our elbows in Jersey?

*(*MITCHELL *is stuffing oddments from bureau into purse.)*

MITCHELL: Our asses in the Village that's all I know. Only, you never see that kid.

CRANK: I never see her.

MITCHELL: You did not geeze her ass.

CRANK: Would I shoot up a minor?

*(*BLOW *stares at bathroom door.)*

BLOW: Ricky? *(Pause)* Ricky hey. *(He crosses to bathroom door.)*

MITCHELL: *(To* CRANK*)* You was workin', where was you workin' last night?

CRANK: The Haymarket?

MITCHELL: Who saw you?

CRANK: The bartender?

*(*BLOW *opens bathroom door, looks inside. Abruptly* BLOW *closes bathroom door; stares at it.)*

MITCHELL: *(Still rummaging.)* Yesterday I was so suckin' relieve I miss the gang bang at Bryant Park? Now I wish they'd a ka-fucking arrested me. Blow, you hear they got that Black Maria now drive right inna park? They drag you in there kick the shit outa you hand you a summons. One J and they drag you in there. Two pounds a scag you can diddle a cop you can fuckin' diddle the schmucky mayor. But one loose J they drag you in there and rip out your pussy. Yesterday I wish they woulda.

CRANK: *(To* MITCHELL*)* Christopher Street? How we gonna deal for shit on Christopher? That's sissy that's poopie.

MITCHELL: *(Pausing)* Blow?

*(*BLOW *turns and crosses slowly to bed. He begins to straighten sheet around body. Finds T-shirt. Stares at it)*

MITCHELL: Blow?

*(*BLOW *stuffs T-shirt in his back pocket. Looks at body)*

BLOW: *(Still looking at body; to* MITCHELL*)* Don't worry about Ricky no more.

(Pause)

MITCHELL: Ka-fuck.

*(*BLOW *crosses to entrance door and wordlessly exits.)*

MITCHELL: Hey. Blow. See you downtown? *(Pause)* Come on, Crank, let's get our titties in gear. You leave anything this apartment?

CRANK: What do Blow mean don't worry about Ricky?

MITCHELL: What Blow means is don't worry about Ricky. Anybody ask, he's asleep on the toilet. Like today ditn't happen. Hey. Crank. Where is Ricky?

CRANK: Asleep on the toilet, last night I leave him passed out on the toilet.

MITCHELL: Where?

CRANK: Asleep on the toilet?

*(*MITCHELL *turns from bureau, looks about room. Crosses to bed; switches sheet away, exposing* JOHN ANTHONY's *naked body.)*

MITCHELL: Give those undercover cunts a thrill. Where, Crank?

CRANK: On the toilet?

MITCHELL: Where the fuck was you all day?

CRANK: Fifty-third and Third?

MITCHELL: Where?

CRANK: A Toyota a Datsun and a Buick convertible?

MITCHELL: Who inna Buick convertible would pick you up?

CRANK: A Mazda?

(Exit MITCHELL *and* CRANK *through entrance door. Their voices can still be heard offstage.)*

MITCHELL: Where's Ricky?

CRANK: Asleep on the toilet, Mitchell.

MITCHELL: Where?

CRANK: The cocksuckin' toilet!

(Lights up on the body)

SLOW CURTAIN

GLOSSARY

The idiom employed in the play is special to the New York streets or, in some instances, an outright invention of the author. A glossary to the slang and local references most used is here provided.

"blow": Cocaine

"crank": Low-grade methedrine (speed)

"to cack": To die; East Coast slang for giving up the ghost, "cacking", or vomiting up the spirit

"fetus": A very young, innocent child. In other words, a mere unformed baby

"Forty-deuce" specifically refers to Forty-second Street, but is generic for the entire Times Square area, the world's most vital wholesale/retail center for the sex and drug industries

"fuck": The most serviceable word on the New York streets, employed as noun, verb, or adjective. It is used, of course, in its traditional Anglo-Saxon sense, but also as a general expletive; to indicate absolute nullity; to replace milder four-letter words; etc. The phrase used by RICKY—"What you fuck?"—is an uninflected challenge meaning "Where do you get off?/Who do you think you are?"

"to geeze": To inject drugs intravenously

"guinea/greaser": Ethnic slurs; a person of Italian extraction

Local References

The Haymarket: An Eighth Avenue bar famed in the Times Square area, frequented by youthful male hustlers, their johns and pimps.

Tompkins Square: BLOW's home territory, on the Lower East Side of Manhattan, where Ukrainians have long been in conflict with blacks and Puerto Ricans.

East New York: Where RICKY and CRANK hail from, a tough, generally white section of Brooklyn.

Boro Park: In Queens, a Hasidic area, rigidly straight and straitlaced; a Jewish queen's nightmare.

Port Authority: The vast Manhattan bus terminal through which most runaways are likely to pass.

Sixth Avenue: Shorthand for the Avenue of the Americas, in midtown Manhattan; corporate heart of the nation.

Dixie Hotel: Once famous, now defunct hotel where more sedate johns entertained ladies and boys.

Bryant Park: Attached to the Public Library on Forty-second Street, on and off a thriving drug retail market.

SHARON AND BILLY

ORIGINAL PRODUCTION

SHARON AND BILLY was first produced by the Manhattan Class Company (Robert LuPone and Bernard Telsey, Executive Directors), opening on 14 October 1988. The cast and creative contributors were:

MOM . . . . Sonja Lanzener
DAD . . . . Richard Grusin
SHARON . . . . Marisa Tomei
BILLY . . . . Mathew Vipond

Director . . . . W D Cantler
Set design . . . . Gregory Mercurio
Lighting design . . . . John Hastings
Costume design . . . . Sam Fleming
Sound design . . . . John Wise
Production manager . . . . Laura Kravets
Casting . . . . Laurel Smith
Stage manager . . . . Lori Culhane
Co-producer . . . . Maggie Lear
Associate producer . . . . Rona Carr

CHARACTERS & SETTING

MOM, *in her thirties*
DAD, *in his forties*
SHARON, *fifteen, aging to seventeen*
BILLY, *thirteen, aging to fifteen*

TIME

The late 1950s
The time span covered is nearly two years.

SETTING

A single set. The dining room of a blue-collar tract home in a suburb of Los Angeles. Beige walls, chartreuse full-length drapes. Portrait in flocked velvet of a Mexican peasant on one wall. Dining-room table, chairs, and cabinet in the debased "Danish modern" of the period. Door to kitchen, off right; doorway to front room, off left. Across back wall, when drapes drawn, a sliding plate glass door through which is visible a sterile backyard patio and a wretched evergreen elm. The dining room is dominated by the dinner table.

Scene One: Dinnertime
Scene Two: Late afternoon, a month later
Scene Three: Dinnertime, three months later
Scene Four: Saturday afternoon, six months later
Scene Five: Evening, six months later
Scene Six: Dinnertime, three months later
Scene Seven: Morning, two weeks later

A NOTE ON THE MUSIC

Some very evocative R & B of the l950s is used to bridge the scenes of this play. Their placement is specific. Only the first eight to fifteen bars of each song need be played. The songs are as follows:

Opening: "Sincerely" by the Moonglows (Chess, 1581)
1-2: "Sh-Boom" by the Chords (Cat, 104)
2-3: "Sorry (I Ran All the Way Home)" by the Impalas (Cub, 9022)
3-4: "Little Star" by the Elegants (Apt, 2500)
4-5: "Love Is Strange" by Mickey & Sylvia (Groove)
5-6: "Daddy's Home" by Shep & the Limelights (Hull, 740)
6-7: "Come On, Let's Go" by Richie Valens (Marna)
Closing: "Speedo" by the Cadillacs (Josie, 785)

Scene One

(A darkened stage)

(Sound track: "Sincerely" by the Moonglows)

(Music fades. Lights up on:)

(Dinnertime. Drapes open. SHARON, *setting table, to* MOM, *in kitchen, off)*

SHARON: *(Frustrated)* Oh, mother.

MOM: What now?

SHARON: I need a fork.

MOM: Ignatz.

SHARON: And a knife.

*(*MOM *enters; as she hands* SHARON *a fork:)*

MOM: Your father won't like it, it's meat loaf.

SHARON: Never mind.

MOM: What?

SHARON: I needed a *butter* knife.

MOM: I just don't know. *(She exits into the kitchen.)*

SHARON: Oh, mother.

MOM: It's the best I can do. I put onions.

SHARON: Could you bring a spoon?

MOM: Eighty cents a pound for steak. Jeesh.

SHARON: Mother?

(Reenter MOM *with glasses and a butter knife.)*

MOM: Or creamed tuna. Your father won't eat creamed tuna.

SHARON: *(Taking butter knife)* Mother, you won't forget?

MOM: It's too easy to fix, that's why.

SHARON: *(Sarcastic)* Billy likes creamed tuna.

MOM: That's *all* he likes.

(Exit MOM *into kitchen.)*

SHARON: Oh, mother.

MOM: Ignatz.

SHARON: I need *another* spoon. *(She exits into kitchen; as she does so:)* Mother, you won't forget to ask Daddy?

MOM: *(Ignoring her; fussing)* Jeesh.

(Enter BILLY *from front room, left. He sits at table.)*

BILLY: Mom?

MOM: Hmmmm?

(Reenter SHARON, *with spoon and plates.)*

BILLY: What's for dinner?

SHARON: *(Hissing)* Slugs.

MOM: Meat loaf.

BILLY: *(To* SHARON*)* Shut up. *(To himself)* I hate meat loaf.

SHARON: *(Mimics him)* "I hate meat loaf."

BILLY: *(Staring at plate)* This ain't my plate. Mine got dividers!

SHARON: *(Exasperated)* Sorry. *(Calling to* MOM; *singsong)* Mother? I forgot Billy's special plate so his peas don't get mixed in with his mashed po-taaa-toes!

BILLY: Shut up.

MOM: Sharon? Go wake up your father and turn off the T V.

SHARON: Billy, go wake Daddy up.

BILLY: I think he's dead.

SHARON: Dead men don't snore.

BILLY: It's the vibrating chair.

SHARON: Mother, you won't forget?

MOM: *(To sound of spoon against rim of pan)* Go wake your father up. Jeesh. I hate to cook.

BILLY: He died and no one will notice. He'll rot in the vibrating chair, his mouth open like this, and we'll all think he's snoring. But he's dead.

SHARON: Good. Then I can go to the sock hop.

BILLY: At Skate-O-Rama? All those hoods?

SHARON: *(Sarcastic)* No, not at Skate-O-Rama. *(Grins)* Maybe I'll go to Memphis!

BILLY: Where?

SHARON: Where Elvis lives, dummie! *(Shimmies shoulders, sings first verse of "Heartbreak Hotel")*

BILLY: *(Watching her; eagerly)* We could drive there. When I get my car.

SHARON: *(Giggling)* A Billymobile,

BILLY: I'm gonna paint these brodie flames. All over it!

SHARON: *(Snapping fingers)* Yeah!

BILLY: It'll be the cherriest car in Memphis!

SHARON: *(Shimmies)* They got pink Cadillacs!

BILLY: We could burn rubber! All the way to Memphis!

SHARON: They got sock hops every night!

BILLY: Just you and me. Peelin' out!

(He makes motor noises)

SHARON: I could have Elvis's baby!

BILLY: And never come back!

(They laugh.)

(Abruptly, SHARON stops laughing, resumes setting table.)

SHARON: You're not invited. Elvis don't like brains.

BILLY: Oh yeah? So poop on your sock hops. I know where you're going. *(Mimics radio announcer; contemptuously)* "Be there or be square".

SHARON: *You're* square.

BILLY: *(Same)* "All your old girlfriends'll be there, all your old boyfriends'll be there. Every greasy low-rider, every—"

(SHARON jabs BILLY's shoulder sharply with her knuckle.)

SHARON: Be quiet!

BILLY: Ouch! *(Lower)* "El! Monte! Legion! Staaa-dium!"

SHARON: Billy! He'll hear you.

BILLY: Dad don't even like it when you watch Johnny Otis.

SHARON: Johnny Otis is cool!

BILLY: *(Mimics DAD)* "Nigger music."

SHARON: R 'n B is cool, so shut up.

BILLY: What'll you gimme?

SHARON: *(Arch)* Reefer.

BILLY: *(Shocked)* Huh?

SHARON: Stupid.

(Enter MOM *with meat loaf.)*

MOM: Where's your father?

BILLY: I'll get him, Mom.

(Exit BILLY, *left.)*

*(*MOM *begins slicing meat loaf onto plates that* SHARON *passes her.)*

MOM: *(Pausing)* It's awful. I put all these onions in.

SHARON: *(Sarcastic)* Daddy loves onions.

MOM: *(Resuming)* It tastes like onions. I don't care what he says! Go get Billy's plate.

SHARON: *(Into kitchen)* When'll you ask him?

MOM: *(Calling after her)* Don't make a federal case.

(Enter DAD *and* BILLY.)

(Enter SHARON *with* BILLY's *plate.)*

MOM: *(To* DAD, *hastily)* Sharon wants to go out tonight. A dance.

DAD: No.

(All sit.)

(They pass food around and eat in silence.)

DAD: *(To his wife)* It's good, sweetie.

MOM: About two pounds of onions.

BILLY: *(Picking at food)* I hate onions. *(Beat; to his mother, sarcastically:)* Sweetie.

DAD: *(To* BILLY) Eat.

SHARON: *(Tearing into her meal)* It's a sock hop. Brenda's going. And Cheryl.

DAD: *(To* SHARON; *through his food)* Don't get on your high horse.

SHARON: But, Daddy.

DAD: You been out.

SHARON: Yeah, but—

DAD: *(Mimics her)* "Yeahbut. Yeahbut." Don't yeahbut me. *(Eats)* Every Friday and Saturday night for umpteen weeks. *(Chuckles)* You'll wear holes in your socks all these sock hops.

SHARON: Oh, Daddy.

DAD: You're always goin' off someplace! Remember we usta go drivin' in my pickup? Me and my girl and I'd show you stuff. Drove you everywhere.

BILLY: Watts is all I got.

MOM: *(Warning)* Billy.

BILLY: All I got was you'd drive around Watts and yell about the Negroes.

DAD: That's cause you was always such a pill! All you did was complain about the dirt in my pickup! *(Pokes food in mouth; to SHARON)* But you, I'd show you all the places we was puttin' in pipelines. You usta like that. So stay home for once. *(Sentimental)* With your pore old man.

SHARON: *(Under breath)* Shit.

DAD: What did you say?

MOM: The potatoes, honey, they're au gratin, did—

(DAD slams knife and fork on table, rattling the dishes; SHARON recoils)

MOM: —you notice?

(DAD stares at his daughter, who cowers. Silence. He resumes eating.)

(BILLY surreptitiously pinches SHARON under table as:)

DAD: Listenin' to monkey music and gallavantin' around. Fifteen years old and what? Slings her hips all these petticoats, and now these see-through blouses!

BILLY: *(Plucking at his chest)* Peek-a-boo.

DAD: *(To BILLY)* Shut up. *(To MOM; indicating SHARON with fork)* She can't get into stewardess school lookin' like that!

BILLY: *(Snickering)* Stewardess.

MOM: I know, honey.

DAD: *(Pointing at SHARON)* This is not! American Airlines over here!

MOM: No, dear.

BILLY: *I'm* gonna be a rich and famous artist!

MOM: Or a teacher.

DAD: *(Same)* This! Is a Greyhound Bus to Tijuana, is what this is!

MOM: Oh, now.

BILLY: Big old pictures, Dad, a mile long!

DAD: *(To BILLY)* Yeah, on the walls of a nuthouse somewhere! *(To SHARON)* Breasts like you got shouldn't be on display. *(Points with fork)* This is like. A cellophane package! Of boobs.

MOM: Honey.

SHARON: All the girls wear these!

DAD: All the girls don't got boobs like you! You walk around like that, you're askin' for it. You could get hurt or somethin'.

BILLY: Why?

(Beat)

DAD: *(Staring at his son)* What?

BILLY: If you like a girl's boobs, why would you hurt 'em?

MOM: Stop saying "boobs."

DAD: *(Pointing at BILLY's plate)* This here is your special plate, right?

BILLY: Yeah?

DAD: So eat out of it! *(Eating. To MOM)* When I was a kid? Back in Chicago? If I saw some girl in this here? I'd'a reached for those things and played basketball with 'em.

BILLY: *Basketball?*

DAD: *(Ignoring this; to MOM)* It's a provocation, these soft things like this bouncin' around in public. I wouldn't blame some kid if he—

(Suddenly, he playfully reaches out for SHARON; she recoils.)

SHARON: Daddy!

MOM: Honey, stop it!

DAD: *(Withdrawing hand; laughing)* Well, she's askin' for it!

BILLY: *(Poking SHARON under table)* Basketball!

MOM: Honey, we should at least let her throw a party. A few kids—

DAD: What? In *my* house? A buncha hoods? Laying around *my* house?

MOM: A few of the nicer kids, honey—

DAD: You know what you're sayin'? The way boys are today? You want 'em swaggerin' around here actin' like animals? Fulla acne and with switchblades?

MOM: Now, they don't have switchblades.

DAD: Drippin' hair grease all over our rugs?

MOM: It's the *style*, honey.

BILLY: Yeah, like Dennis.

SHARON: *(Kicking BILLY under table)* Shut up.

DAD: I can't even look at 'em when they come by to pick her up. *(Jabs fork in SHARON's direction)* And she wants to stay out past eleven.

SHARON: Cheryl gets to stay out past midnight.

DAD: At midnight those greaseballs turn into werewolves! I should make it ten.

SHARON: Daddy!

MOM: But if we let her have a party, we'd be here to supervise. They could stay later and have games and—

(DAD *jabs fork into piece of meat. Lifts it*)

DAD: Who put this here?

(MOM *shakes her head.*)

DAD: (*Pointing about him with impaled meat*) Who put the T V out there? Who put clothes on these kids? Who put the money in your hand for those green drapes?

MOM: Chartreuse, honey.

DAD: *Who did that?*

MOM: I know.

(DAD *drops meat on plate.*)

DAD: No hoody dirtheads gonna party in here and put their greasy hands on stuff I worked hard for.

SHARON: (*Under breath*) Wouldn't hurt your old stuff.

DAD: (*To* SHARON) What's your old man do?

(*No response*)

DAD: What does he do all day?

SHARON: It's the biggest sock hop of the year!

DAD: Construction! I'm a foreman in that hot sun, and I got skin problems! We just put in. Fifty inch. A fifty-inch pipeline in Laguna Beach. While you! Are runnin' around niggered up with all this— (*Mimics Chuck Berry style guitar, grotesquely*) —TWANG-A-BWANG-A-THUMP-A-THUMP—

(BILLY *joins in under this.*)

BILLY: Rang. A dang. A rang—

MOM: (*Quickly*) Harry Belafonte!

(*Abrupt silence, as* DAD *stares at* MOM)

MOM: She likes Harry Belafonte too, honey.

DAD: (*Nodding ominously*) Oh. (*Beat*) She does? (*He leans forward.*) And because why? (*No response*) She thinks he's. Cute.

SHARON: (*Low tones*) He is cute.

DAD: Negroes. Ain't. Cute. You can say they're decent-lookin' sometimes. But never *cute*.

SHARON: What's the difference?

DAD: There's a difference! Cute is like you wanna kiss him. *(Eats)* You wanna kiss those big lips?

SHARON: Can I be excused?

DAD: Finish your dinner.

SHARON: I'm not hungry.

BILLY: *(Aside to* DAD; *setting him straight)* Harry Belafonte don't have big lips. *Elvis* got big lips.

DAD: *(To* BILLY) Chew on your meat loaf!

(BILLY hastily does so.)

DAD: *(To* SHARON) You too. Eat your dinner. *(She doesn't move.)* Young lady? *(No response)* I said eat. *(Ominous)* Young. Lady.

SHARON: *(In one breath)* Billy was smoking in the car when we washed it Saturday, and he burned that hole in the seat cover!

MOM: Sharon Ann!

(Beat, as SHARON *picks up fork, jabs food in her mouth)*

(BILLY stabs at SHARON *under table with fork.)*

DAD: *(To* BILLY) You been smokin'? *(No response)* *(To his wife)* Jesus. What a pair of kids we got.

MOM: *(Angry)* She shouldn't tell tales.

DAD: *(To* BILLY) I catch you smokin' and I'll tan your butt. So don't do it again.

BILLY: *(Flip)* O K.

DAD: O K, *who*?

BILLY: *(Military)* O K, *sir*.

DAD: That's better.

(They eat in silence.)

(SHARON and BILLY glare at each other)

SHARON: *(Exasperated; suddenly giggling)* Elvis. Got. Big. Lips.

(BILLY giggles)

(MOM smiles, then laughs)

(DAD looks at them, then smiles. He raises his hand in mock anger at BILLY.)

(BILLY beams.)

(They all laugh.)

(Suddenly, at the peak of their laughter:)

(Blackout)

(Soundtrack: The opening bars of "Sh-Boom" by the Chords)

(Music continues into:)

Scene Two

(Afternoon, a month later. Drapes and plate glass doors opened wide. Hot white sunlight.)

(Table is a mess of luncheon remains: a ravaged loaf of Wonder bread, opened jars of peanut butter, jelly, mayonnaise; a pried-open can of Nestle's chocolate syrup, a package of franks, milk carton, dirty glasses, cookies, sandwich rinds.)

(Under music, SHARON runs shrieking into dining room from backyard. She wears a tight, two-piece period bathing suit, which covers her adolescent hips and breasts like bands of shiny steel.)

(A spray of water from offstage. Music out on:)

SHARON: Safety zone!

(BILLY appears in backyard, wearing trunks, dripping wet, holding lawn hose stoppered with finger.)

BILLY: Take your medicine!

SHARON: No. *(Circling table)*

(BILLY releases a jet of water into dining room.)

SHARON: Billy! Not in here!

(BILLY discards hose, enters dining room.)

BILLY: So? What do you care?

SHARON: Just don't, that's all. *(Sits, digs into food)* God. I'm still hungry.

BILLY: What do you care? Mom and Dad'll be in Palm Springs the whole weekend.

SHARON: *(Angrily buttering bread)* Yeah, and I should be too.

BILLY: Then you shouldn't'a snuck out to that sock hop with Dennis.

SHARON: Tough shitsky.

BILLY: After Dad said you couldn't! Two o'clock in the morning!

SHARON: So tough shitsky.

BILLY: *(Mimics)* "Tough shitsky." You *sound* like Dennis.

SHARON: Wish he was here.

BILLY: Dennis been grounded too, ha-ha.

SHARON: Wish it was anybody but *you.*

BILLY: *I* ain't grounded for two whole months, ha-ha.

SHARON: You shoulda been! Dad caught you reading those *National Geographics* in the bathroom!

BILLY: I'm supposed to know anatomy! For art class. *(Sits, digs in)* He was only mad for a minute.

SHARON: *(Disdainfully)* Anatomy. *(Giggles)* All those naked Negroes, what a nurdie.

BILLY: *(Airily)* I coulda gone to Palm Springs if I wanted. I can always go where I want.

SHARON: Goody for you.

BILLY: Only I just hate Palm Springs. All those old golfcarts and fat people.

SHARON: *(Angrily eating)* I coulda gone horseback riding. Swimming. I got a new bathing suit.

BILLY: We'll have fun anyway.

SHARON: No, we won't.

BILLY: *(Impish)* Bread balls.

SHARON: Huh?

BILLY: Like this.

(He takes slice of white bread, extracts the soft center, wads it in fist, rolls it into ball on table.)

SHARON: *(Giggling)* Put some jelly. *(She extends knife with blob of jelly on it)*

BILLY: No. Peanut butter. *(He dips ball in jar of peanut butter.)*

SHARON: *And* jelly!

(She smears ball with jelly; he eats it.)

BILLY: *(Laughing through food)* God.

SHARON: Watch. *(She smears bread with mayonnaise.)*

BILLY: Yuckie! A mayonnaise sandwich!

(He watches her eat, her mouth open.)

BILLY: God! You're makin' me sick!

(She eats, bigger.)

BILLY: Sharon! Stop it! O K for you. Look. (*He takes slice of bread, wads it, then squashes and pounds it flat on table.*)

SHARON: What are you doing?

BILLY: Mexican sandwich.

SHARON: A what?

BILLY: Look. (*He lifts flattened bread, dips it in can of chocolate syrup.*)

SHARON: (*Watching him*) What a weirdio!

(BILLY *pops dripping concoction in mouth.*)

BILLY: Yum. Meeee.

SHARON: (*Disgusted*) Dum. Meeee.

BILLY: (*Leaning towards her*) They'd hate it if they saw us!

SHARON: (*Giggling*) Yeah! (*Reaches for milk carton; pours*) Watch. (*She drinks entire glass, the liquid dribbling down chin onto breasts. Finishes with a flourish*) Milkstache!

BILLY: (*Laughing*) What?

SHARON: Dennis *loves* licking off my milkstache. (*She indicates upper lip.*) That's what he calls it. From the milk.

BILLY: (*Contemptuously*) Clev-errrr.

SHARON: Shut up.

BILLY: Watch this. (*He spills a little milk onto table, mixes in some jelly.*)

SHARON: Billy!

BILLY: (*Finger painting*) It's a painting! (*Smears*) This is Dennis' hair. (*Adds cookies*) And his ears. And— (*Takes a weinie*) His nose. (*Takes another*) And down here—

SHARON: Don't be *dirty*! God.

BILLY: So lemme draw *you!*

SHARON: No.

BILLY: I mean a *real* picture. I'm gettin' good, you'll see.

(SHARON *casually brushes milk off breasts and adjusts top of suit as:*)

SHARON: I dunno. Maybe.

BILLY: Please. Pretty please? With mayonnaise on it?

SHARON: (*Fluffing hair*) Oh. I dunno. (*Throws cookie at him*) O K.

BILLY: (*Rising*) I'll get my stuff! (*He exits.*)

(SHARON *licks lips, puts hands to hips, raises shoulders cheese-cake style, and belches.*)

(*Giggling, she leans forward and runs finger through guck on table.*)

(*Reenter* BILLY *with pad and crayons. He sits, crayon poised.*)

BILLY: O K. Pose for me. Something sexy. Something low-rider.

(SHARON *puts finger to cheek, wide-eyed innocence.*)

BILLY: What's that?

SHARON: Annette.

BILLY: Who?

SHARON: Annette Funicello. (*No response; drops pose. No response; finger to cheek*) So draw me.

BILLY: That ain't sexy.

SHARON: So this. (*She spins around, straddling chair; waves.*) Back of a motorcycle.

BILLY: That's a little better. Try something else.

SHARON: O K. (*She rises, sits on edge of table, hugging shoulders. Pouts cutely*) Oooh.

BILLY: What's that? That "oooh"?

SHARON: Models. They all do that. (*Pouts*) Draw it.

BILLY: (*Drawing*) They don't neither. "Oooh."

SHARON: They do too.

BILLY: (*Contemptuously*) Annette Mouseketeer.

SHARON: (*Dropping pose*) Oh, you don't know anything. Here.

(*She leans back onto table, propping herself with palms, among the half-eaten sandwiches, legs crossed, classic bathing beauty pose.*)

BILLY: You keep changing!

SHARON: (*Thrusting up breasts*) Ooooh.

(BILLY *stares.*)

BILLY: Wow. (*Ripping out sheet, starting another*) That's bitchin'. (*Draws*)

SHARON: *Seventeen.*

BILLY: (*Drawing rapidly*) Huh?

SHARON: Someday. I'm gonna be on the cover of *Seventeen.*

BILLY: (*Snickering as he draws*) With those big old knockers?

SHARON: (*Tensing*) Shut up.

BILLY: That's why you're so popular. That's why Dennis likes you.

SHARON: That's mean! (*Abruptly dropping pose, she sits up, crossing arms over her breasts.*)

BILLY: Sharon, stop changing! That was sexy!

SHARON: You're just. I dunno. Stupoid.

BILLY: But it was real low-rider!

SHARON: Yeah, well you're a brain!

BILLY: Who is?

SHARON: (*Taunting*) Everybody at North says. Billy. Is a brain.

BILLY: Am not.

SHARON: Are too.

BILLY: Not!

SHARON: Are.

BILLY: Dad says you're just a greasy, cheap, low-rider Pachuco slut!

(SHARON *springs angrily from table.*)

SHARON: Dennis says you're queer!

(BILLY *freezes.* SHARON *sits, tears into food.*)

BILLY: What?

SHARON: My creepo brother!

BILLY: What. Did Dennis say?

SHARON: Nobody likes you!

(BILLY *discards pad and crayon onto floor, rises.*)

BILLY: God. They catch you reading a book and. (*Crosses to plate glass; looks out*) God.

SHARON: (*Blithely*) You're just a farmer, that's all.

BILLY: No. You.

SHARON: (*Singsong*) Four-eyed farmer and a queerio.

BILLY: Pachuco sluttio.

SHARON: (*Laughing through food*) Brain farmer.

BILLY: (*Also laughing*) Grease rider chiquita.

SHARON: (*Same*) Teacher pet face.

BILLY: (*Same*) Mexi-nose.

SHARON: *Let's draw Dad!*

BILLY: Bitchin'! *(She springs for drawing stuff on floor and scoots under table.)*

(BILLY joins her.)

SHARON: *(Giggling; drawing)* In his undershirt.

BILLY: *(Taking pad and crayon)* No, Sharon. Like this. See?

SHARON: *(Watching him draw)* Yeah. In the vibrating chair.

BILLY: Yeah. Or this.

SHARON: What's—?

BILLY: Like when he walks around the house naked.

(She grabs pad away.)

SHARON: Not that. Not dirty.

BILLY: O K. O K. *(Retrieves pad; draws)* In his work boots. Scratching himself. Skin problems.

SHARON: Give him green spots.

BILLY *And this is you.*

SHARON *Huh?*

BILLY: As a stewardess. Dad's in a plane in a vibrating seat and you're serving him coffee and this— *(Crayon slides off pad onto her knee)* —is the Rockies. You're flyin' over the Rockies.

SHARON *(Giggling)* Where we going?

BILLY: To Memphis. To marry Elvis. And so you keep flying— *(Crayon up her thigh)*

SHARON: That tickles, dummie!

BILLY: And flying and now you're over— *(Crayon stright up her hip, midriff, to breasts)* The Grand Tetons!

SHARON *Stop it!*

(Crayon jumps to her shoulder.)

BILLY: O K! The pretty hills of Nebraska and— *(Along her shoulder to clavicle and up her neck)* The beautiful Colorado gorge and— *(To her mouth)* The Black Hole of Kansas!

(SHARON grabs crayon and colors his nose.)

SHARON: And this is Albuquerque!

BILLY: O K, where else?

(Crayon down his chin, neck)

SHARON: And this is Chicken Neck, Arkansas—

BILLY: *(Giggling)* Shut up.

(Crayon down shoulders and chest)

SHARON: And Chicken Wing, Tennessee, and Chicken Ribs, North Dakota—

BILLY: Keep going.

(Crayon to his belly)

SHARON: Little Pot, Montana, and—

(He pushes crayon downward.)

BILLY: And that's where Elvis lives!

(Shocked, she drops crayon.)

SHARON: Billy! You shouldn't do that *in public!*

(She turns away as he quickly draws up his legs.)

SHARON: God. You're worse than Dennis.

BILLY: *(Delighted)* I am?

SHARON: Least he tries to *hide* his.

BILLY: Really?

SHARON: God. *(She starts doodling on pad.)*

BILLY: It felt good, that's all. *(Beat)* I'm sorry.

SHARON: Shut up and report to the vice principal.

BILLY: What you drawing?

SHARON: Nothing. I'm dreaming

BILLY: What about?

SHARON: Oh. A beautiful place.

BILLY: That's nice. Boy. *(He props his chin on her shoulder.)* I'd rather be with you. Than anybody.

(Beat; she doodles on, her head against his.)

SHARON: Billy?

BILLY: Hmmm?

SHARON: Dad didn't really. Call me a slut. Did he?

BILLY: Dad. He got rocks in his head.

SHARON: He said that? Right out loud?

BILLY: He was just mad you stayed out so late. *(Beat)* You're the best sister in California.

(SHARON closes her eyes, hums a dance tune, languidly doodles.)

SHARON: I can see a sock hop palace.

BILLY: Yeah? And what else?

SHARON: All these kids. Laughing. And me in the middle. Dancing.

(She hums softly, eyes closed, his head on her shoulder.)

BILLY: With me, Sharon? Would you dance with me?

(She ceases to hum. Opens her eyes. Tears are welling.)

SHARON: I'm not. A slut.

(SHARON reaches out blindly for her brother, who hugs her to him.)

(Clutching at each other, they sink full-length onto the floor, a tangle of awkward limbs.)

(Lights slowly dim to black as:)

(Sound track: the opening bars of "Sorry (I Ran All the Way Home)" by the Impalas)

(Music fades. Lights up on:)

Scene Three

(Dinnertime, three months later. Drapes partially drawn)

(MOM is sitting at table, head in hands, SHARON sitting across from her. Sheepishly:)

SHARON: Oh, mother. *(Silence)* Say something. *(Silence. Groping:)* I can't. This is. *(Silence)* Yell at me. Say you hate me or. *(Silence)* You hate me.

MOM: You. *Ignatz! (She rises, turns, sits down again, face in hands.)* I could use. A filthy word.

SHARON: I guess you should say it.

MOM: Your father. Will go through the roof.

SHARON: Yell at me. I would. If I was you.

MOM: *(Looking at daughter)* How would you know?

SHARON: What?

MOM: What I feel. How would— *(Pause)* —you know?

SHARON: I can't say I'm sorry fifty times.

MOM: I don't believe it.

SHARON: Maybe she's wrong.

MOM: *(Hastily)* The school nurse? What did she say?

SHARON: I told you.

MOM: Oh. *(Beat)* We could. Wait. For the tests.

SHARON: We don't have to tell Daddy now.

MOM: No.

SHARON: Do we?

(MOM rises, exits into kitchen.)

(SHARON fidgets.)

MOM: *(From kitchen)* Which one was it? Sharon? *(She reenters with coffee cup.)* You see so many boys. Was it Dennis?

SHARON: I guess so.

MOM: You guess?

SHARON: Yes. Dennis.

MOM: How. Many. Boys. Have you. *(She plops into chair.)* Through the roof.

(They sit staring in silence.)

(Enter BILLY, left. Throws books on table)

BILLY: *(Spluttering like a souped-up auto)* Tuck 'n roll. *(Gear shift sound)* Taco balls. *(Peeling tires sound)* The Marquis.

(BILLY exits into kitchen.)

(MOM and SHARON sit in silence.)

BILLY: *(From kitchen)* Mom? Next year I get a car, right?

MOM: *(Dully)* Right.

BILLY: *(Sticking his head out of kitchen)* Right?

MOM: *(Angrily)* Right!

BILLY: *(Same)* O K. O K. You don't haveta bite my face off. *(Disappears into kitchen. From there:)* Dad looked at this '54 Chevy I don't want that. A '56 maybe. That's cherry. I could get into a car club with that. *(Re-enters with sandwich, sits)* A plaque. See it through the rear window. The Marquis. Or the Monarchs.

SHARON: The Creeps.

MOM: Sharon!

(SHARON looks at her mother, then at BILLY.)

SHARON: *(Mimics her brother)* "The Monarchs." Fat chance.

BILLY: Shut up.

(SHARON begins to giggle, a tad hysterically.)

SHARON: "The Marquis, the Monarchs." Who would cruise with *you*?
You and some skag. Two fudds in some old '54 Chevy. "The Fudds."
You could join "The Fudds." Two four-eyed-creepo-scaggy-*brains*!
(*She bangs fist on table; covers face with hands.*)

(MOM *and* BILLY *stare at her.*)

MOM: Sharon *Ann*!

BILLY: God. What did *I* do?

MOM: (*To* BILLY) Go out and play.

BILLY: Go out and play what?

MOM: (*Ominously*) Go. Read. A book.

(SHARON *looks at ceiling; a curt laugh.*)

SHARON: Yeah. A book.

(BILLY *gazes from one to the other, puts half-eaten sandwich in mouth,
gathers up books.*)

BILLY: (*Looking at them; through sandwich*) God.

(*Exit* BILLY, *left.*)

(*Silence*)

MOM: We could say, maybe. But we're not sure yet.

SHARON: (*Shaking her head*) Oh, mother.

MOM: And Dennis' parents. We'll have to talk to them.

SHARON: (*Same*) Stop.

MOM: We'll have to send you back east. Your grandmother.

SHARON: I don't care.

MOM: That. Is. Obvious. (*Rises, turns to enter kitchen, pauses*)
I should fix something. For dinner. I should fix. Liver.

SHARON: (*Toneless*) And onions.

MOM: Lots of onions.

SHARON: (*Bitterly sarcastic*) Billy hates onions.

MOM: He can eat a frozen. How many, Sharon?

SHARON: What?

MOM: How many boys? (*No response*) You tell your father. Only Dennis.

SHARON: That's. Cootie.

MOM: That's what?

SHARON: Not fair.

MOM: Does Dennis know about. Any other boys?

SHARON: *(Quickly)* No.

MOM: Then *only Dennis.* You better tell him that.

(MOM exits into kitchen.)

(SHARON sits in silence, smoothing her petticoats.)

(Sound of a door slamming)

(SHARON hastily rises, exits into kitchen.)

(Enter DAD, in soiled work clothes, carrying tin lunch pail. He is tired.)

DAD: *(Calling)* Sweetheart?

MOM: *(From kitchen)* Take a bath.

DAD: *(Sitting; lunch pail on table)* Gimme a whiskey and water first.

MOM: O K.

DAD: *(Afterthought)* Sweetie.

MOM: O K.

(He lights cigarette, exhales slowly, begins untying caked workman's boots—all punctuated with groans of fatigue.)

(MOM enters with drink.)

DAD: *(Taking drink)* Oh, woman. You don't know. *(Drinks deeply, sounds of pleasure)*

MOM: Honey, um.

DAD: *(Looking at her)* You been crying?

MOM: Chopping onions. We're having liver and onions.

DAD: Hey now. Is that right? I'll be goddamned.

MOM: You can't even see the liver. All those onions.

DAD: *(Rubbing hands together)* Goddamn. Ol' Dad gets his favorite. *(Beat)* Why?

MOM: What?

DAD: Well, *somethin's* gotta be wrong. I get my favorite.

(MOM laughs nervously.)

(Beat)

MOM: There is.

DAD: So?

(Beat)

MOM: After dinner.

DAD: I said: So?

MOM: We'll talk later.

DAD: Sharon or Billy?

MOM: Sharon. After dinner, honey. We'll talk.

DAD: Where is she?

MOM: In the kitchen.

(DAD rises.)

MOM: Leave her alone.

(He stares at her; sits.)

DAD: Bring her in here. *(Beat)* Now.

(MOM hesitates, then exits into kitchen.)

(DAD places lunch pail on floor and clasps his hands before him, waiting.)

(MOM reenters, SHARON slowly following.)

DAD: *(To SHARON)* Well, young lady. *(Silence)* I said. Well, young lady.

SHARON: I heard you.

(Pause)

DAD: You heard me. Good. *(To his wife)* She heard me. *(To SHARON)* So answer me.

MOM: Honey.

DAD: Let her tell it.

MOM: It happens, honey, it's—

DAD: *(Banging table)* Shut up! Let. Her. Tell it.

MOM: She's ignatz.

(DAD stares at MOM.)

DAD: *(Grotesquely mimics his wife)* "She's ignatz! She's ignatz!"

MOM: Honey, don't get—

DAD: *(Gesturing wildly)* "Ignatz! Ignatz!"

SHARON: *(Quickly)* I'm gonna—!

(DAD ceases, stares at his daughter.)

SHARON: Gonna have a baby.

(Pause)

DAD: You. What?

SHARON: I told you.

DAD: Say it again. I didn't hear this.

MOM: (Dropping into a chair) The high school nurse, honey. Only.
There's no tests. I mean—

DAD: I didn't *hear* this!

SHARON: Oh, Daddy.

DAD: (To SHARON) You let some boy. Put his. Up *you*? (Beat; he leans across
table towards her.) Is that what you said? (Beat) You said. Some boy. Put his.
His filthy. Up *you*? (Beat) You said that, right? (No response; he draws back.)
Jesus Christ.

(They all stare down at table.)

MOM: We'll send her to your mother's. In Chicago. We'll put it up for
adoption.

DAD: Like a dog. (Beat) I work like a dog. (Looks up at SHARON) You know
what that means? (No response) No, you don't. It means. (Springing to his feet;
loudly) That I got Mexicans all day! (Sits again; gestures helplessly) Means we
hadda dig a ditch today. Uphill. Twenny-four inch pipeline San Onofre. Up!
Hill! (Waves his hand, indicating house) To give you all this.

MOM: (Jumping up) Liver's burning.

(MOM hastily exits into kitchen.)

DAD: (Continuing to SHARON) And you walk up to me. And you squat here.
And crap. All over. (Beat) I come home from work and there's this crap on
my table.

MOM: (From kitchen) Sharon? Set the table.

(SHARON goes in and out of kitchen, setting table, DAD watching her.
As she reenters:)

DAD: Some hood I'll bet. One of those hoods you go out with.

(She exits; reenters.)

DAD: Duck-butt. Right? Pimples.

(She exits; reenters.)

DAD: You like that. Pimples. (Beat) Answer me!

(SHARON stands still, not looking at him.)

(MOM hastily reenters, spatula in hand.)

MOM: Dennis. It was that Dennis.

DAD: That who?

MOM: Blond kid. Drives that candy apple.

(Exit MOM *into kitchen.)*

DAD: *(To* SHARON; *contemptuously)* Den. Nis.

*(*SHARON *exits into kitchen.)*

*(*DAD *drains his whiskey and water.)*

*(*MOM *reenters, coffee pot in hand.)*

MOM: You want coffee?

DAD: This Dennis. Has gotta marry her.

MOM: *(Filling his cup)* They're too young, honey. Your mother's. Back east.

*(*SHARON *reenters, setting table.* DAD *watches her.)*

DAD: Your boyfriend. Is gonna have to drop outa school. Get himself a job. And pay for this.

MOM: Honey, that's—

DAD: *And pay for this! (Beat)* Where's the cream?

MOM: I'll get it.

DAD: No! Sharon's gonna get it. *(To* SHARON*)* Get it.

*(*SHARON, *on verge of tears, exits into kitchen.)*

MOM: How can she marry him? What can he do, he's a kid like her?

DAD: Quiet.

MOM: *We'll* end up supporting them.

DAD: I said. Quiet.

(Reenter SHARON. *Extends milk carton to* DAD*)*

DAD: *(To* SHARON*)* Pour it in.

*(*SHARON *shakily pours; spills it.)*

DAD: Uh-oh. You spilt it. *(Beat)* Uh-oh.

*(*SHARON *gestures helplessly with carton, at a loss.)*

DAD: *(Deadly)* So clean it up.

*(*SHARON *closes her eyes, fighting tears.)*

MOM: I'll get a sponge.

DAD: No! Her. *(To* SHARON*)* Get a sponge and clean it up.

(She sets down carton; exits into kitchen.)

MOM: Honey.

(He is staring after SHARON*)*

MOM: It happens.

(He doesn't respond.)

(Reenter SHARON *with sponge; sops up mess, starts to exit.)*

DAD: Hey.

(She pauses, her back to him.)

DAD: I don't want this coffee it's ruint. *(Beat)* Take it away. Get me another cup.

(She turns back to table.)

DAD: You gotta get use to this. A brat on one tittie and a sponge in your hand.

(She takes cup.)

DAD: Get use to it.

(Exit SHARON *with cup.)*

MOM: I'll get— *(Despairingly puts coffee pot on table)* Dinner.

*(*MOM *exits as* SHARON *reenters with clean cup.)*

*(*DAD *watches as* SHARON *replaces cup and tries shakily to pour coffee into it.)*

DAD: You spilt it again! *(She puts down pot; closes eyes.)* I don't believe this. You can't even pour coffee. And you was gonna go. You was gonna go to stewardess school? You woulda flunked out.

(She sets down pot.)

(Reenter MOM *with plate of food.)*

(To SHARON*, pointing at cup)* Girls who whoor around—

MOM: *(Disapproving)* Honey!

DAD: *(To* MOM*)* You got a nicer word for it? *(To* SHARON*; resuming:)* —Should learn to pour coffee!

*(*SHARON *reaches for his cup.)*

DAD: *(To* SHARON*)* Never mind!

*(*MOM *places plate before him)*

DAD: A girl cheap enough to get pregnant is too cheap. To pour my coffee.

MOM: Get Billy, Sharon.

SHARON: Daddy? *(Beat. She can't look at him.)* Stop.

DAD: *(Feigned innocence)* Stop what?

SHARON: Stop it. I'm. I'm sorry. I wish I was dead.

DAD: You're sorry. *(To his wife)* She wishes she was dead. *(To* SHARON*)* I don't wish that. I just wish you wasn't. *(Beat)* So cheap.

SHARON: Please, Daddy.

DAD: You make us cheap? O K. You crap on us? We can live with that. You don't care about us? Fine. But you. *(Points his knife at her)* Don't care about yourself. That's what hurts. *(Looks at plate)* That's what hurts your Daddy.

MOM: Dinner's getting cold. Sharon, go get Billy.

(Exit MOM *into kitchen.)*

SHARON: *(Fighting tears)* I'll never do it again.

DAD: *(Exploding) I for chrissakes hope not!*

(Reenter MOM *with two plates; to her:)*

DAD: Never do it again. That's funny. This daughter we got? She's *cheap*. But she's funny. *(Beat; to* SHARON*)* How many times? *(Beat;* MOM *pauses to stare at* DAD*.)* How many times you do it with him? This Den. Nis pimple. Huh?

MOM: *(Level voice; setting down plates)* Sharon. Call your brother.

DAD: *(Rising from chair) I wanna know! (He collars his daughter; into her face.)* How. Many. Times.

SHARON: *(Struggling against him)* Daddy.

MOM: *(Clenching fists)* Honey? It's time for dinner!

DAD: *(Bearing down on* SHARON*)* Once? Twice?

SHARON: Mother!

MOM: I said it's time for dinner!

DAD: *(Same)* Six times? *(He has* SHARON *painfully by nape of neck.)* I gotta right to know. Fifty? Just nod your head.

MOM: Leave her alone!

DAD: *(Same)* She was goin' to some *sock hop*? Some movie? *(Mimics)* "Bye, Daddy." You say, "Bye, I'm goin' to a football game."

MOM: *(Grabbing his arm)* You're hurting her!

DAD: *(Shrugging off* MOM *; spinning* SHARON *against table)* So it's tough shit, Daddy, tough *(He slaps* SHARON *once.)* —shit— *(Twice)* —Daddy!

*(*MOM *forces herself between them; pushes* DAD *away)*

MOM: This is Sharon! *(Into his face)* You're doing this. To *Sharon*!

*(*MOM *embraces* SHARON*, who is stunned, blinded, tears welling.)*

*(*DAD *stares at them, then abruptly sits, cuts up liver, breathing hard. To them, through his food:)*

DAD: Sit down. Sit. Down. And eat.

(*Enter* BILLY *noisily, making motor sounds.*)

BILLY: Dinner ready yet?

MOM: (*Easing* SHARON *into chair*) It's ready. Come to the table.

(*Looking hard at* DAD, MOM *exits into kitchen.*)

BILLY: (*Approaching table*) Hi, Dad.

(DAD *does not respond; he is shoveling food into his mouth and staring at* SHARON.)

(BILLY *sits at table. Sees food*)

BILLY: Yuckie. *Liver?*

(SHARON *is looking blindly before her.*)

DAD: (*To* SHARON) Eat.

(*She does not respond.*)

DAD: Girls who act cheap gotta eat everything on her plate.

BILLY: *Liver?* God.

(*Enter* MOM *with T V dinner.*)

MOM: (*To* BILLY) Don't get antsy. You get a frozen.

(MOM *seats herself. They all eat in silence, except for* SHARON, *who stares at plate.* DAD *hasn't taken his eyes from her. Through his food:*)

DAD: Girls who get in trouble. Should eat. What we put in front of her.

(SHARON *blindly picks up fork.*)

DAD: I said. Girls who shame her Daddy should eat her dinner.

(SHARON *lifts forkful of onions to her mouth; pauses.*)

DAD: Should put it in her mouth.

(*She does so.*)

DAD: And eat.

(*She chews slowly. Swallows*)

DAD: All of it. (*Beat*) Eat it all. (*Beat*) I wanna see a clean plate. Like the plate was washed. Clean. (*Beat*) You. Are gonna. (*Beat*) Lick it. (*Beat*) Clean.

(SHARON *drops fork, covers her mouth; chokes into napkin.*)

DAD: Hey! I worked hard for that food.

MOM: (*To her husband*) Stop it. Now.

DAD: (*To his wife; still looking at* SHARON) What?

MOM: I said. Stop it.

DAD: (*Looking at his wife; wide-eyed innocence*) But I worked for that. She craps on me and now she throws up my food?

MOM: Just stop it. *Please.*

DAD: Come on, Sharon. Girls like you. You crap and throw up on your Daddies at the same time? Not. Nice. Now try again.

(SHARON *puts down her napkin; slowly, she follows his instructions:*)

DAD: Take your fork. And your knife. Cut the meat. Cut it up. That's right. Now put it in your mouth. Here.

(*He reaches across table for her hand, forces her to gather onions on her fork.*)

DAD: Put some onions with it. Cram some onions in there.

(*He guides fork into her mouth; she does not chew.*)

BILLY: (*Staring*) God.

DAD: (*Withdrawing hand; to* SHARON) Now. Swallow it. (*Beat*) Swallow it all.

(*She attempts to do so, fighting back the sobs.*)

(*She chokes.*)

DAD: (*Warningly*) Don't you do it again! I worked hard for that.

(*She can't help it; upchucks into napkin.*)

DAD: You did it again! You puked on me again! Here.

(*He reaches across table again and grabs her hand.*)

DAD: Now you gotta start all over!

(*Using free hand,* SHARON *stabs the back of his hand with her knife.*)

(DAD *yells, recoiling.*)

DAD: Jesus!

SHARON: (*Screaming*) I hate you!

DAD: (*Holding out hand to his wife*) Look what she did!

(MOM *covers her face with hands.*)

SHARON: (*Same*) You're having me for dinner!

(*She buries her face in her napkin, sobbing.*)

(*A long pause*)

(DAD *rises from chair, rubbing his hand.*)

(*He looks fearfully at his daughter.*)

(*Exit* DAD, *left.*)

(Front door slams, off.)

(Silence)

BILLY: God.

MOM: *(Rising from chair; to BILLY)* Finish your.

(Shaking her head, MOM exits into kitchen.)

(SHARON and BILLY sit in silence.)

BILLY: Sharon? *(Beat)* What did you do? *(Beat)* Huh?

(She manages to stand.)

SHARON: *(Hand over stomach)* My room. Lay down. *(She slowly crosses left.)*

BILLY: God. You musta done something. Bad.

(SHARON pauses at doorway. Turns, hisses at BILLY)

SHARON: *It's yours!*

(Exit SHARON, quickly, left.)

(BILLY stares after her.)

(Blackout)

(Sound track: the opening bars of "Little Star" by the Elegants)

(Music fades. Lights up on:)

Scene Four

(A Saturday afternoon, six months later. Drapes are open, and sunlight floods the room.)

(MOM is setting table for lunch. She is in and out of kitchen. Goes to plate glass door, opens it.)

MOM: *(Calling)* Honeee? Billeee? Lunch!

(She exits into kitchen.)

(Beat)

(DAD and BILLY enter, in greasy clothes, through plate glass door.)

BILLY: *(Looking at greasy hands)* Icky.

DAD: You gotta expect to get dirty workin' on cars. *(Pours himself a drink from bottle on table)* Go wash up.

BILLY: How come we hadda grease it? You just bought it.

DAD: You should care about your machine. Treat it good and it'll run for your whole life.

BILLY: I gotta drive a '54 Chevy 'til I'm *forty*?

DAD: *(Drinking)* It was a good buy. For the money. Kid like you it's O K.

BILLY: *(Muttering)* A '56 woulda been O K.

(BILLY exits into kitchen.)

DAD: *(Calling after him)* You wanted some M G like that Becker kid? Who's a spoiled rotten snotface?

(Enter MOM with sandwiches; to her:)

DAD: It's not good enough.

MOM: It's a car.

DAD: For the money? It's a great car.

MOM: It's a car. He can drive to Hollywood. And the beach.

DAD: Hollywood? Downey ain't good enough?

MOM: *(Deprecating)* Honey.

DAD: Sunset Strip for chrissakes and then what?

MOM: Go wash your hands.

DAD: It's a good car.

MOM: I know that. Billy's different, that's all.

DAD: He's what?

MOM: That's all. He's more serious.

DAD: Than what?

MOM: Than Sharon. And other kids. He's brainier.

DAD: *(Laughing bitterly)* Hell, Sharon got brains. Only they're between her boobies. Which is why—

MOM: So he's different, that's all.

DAD: She's back east havin' a kid.

MOM: Be quiet. Billy.

DAD: He knows. Everybody knows. *(Points at sandwiches)* That better not be Spam.

MOM: It's ham. Ham and liverwurst. He could be a teacher. He gets very good grades.

DAD: Except in math. He's a boneskull in math. Now Sharon? *(Raises his glass)* Coulda gone to airline school. You know what that means? She coulda flown around like a queen. *(Drains glass; grabs a sandwich)* For free. With benefits.

MOM: Wash your hands.

DAD: *(Munching)* It's the wave of the future. People flyin' to New Jersey like we drive to Covina. And this! She passes up.

MOM: She can still apply. Later.

DAD: She better straighten up back there.

MOM: She can still graduate with her class it's all fixed.

DAD: Airlines ain't gonna hire some girl that screws around.

MOM: I said be quiet.

DAD: You gotta be spotless.

MOM: They won't know.

DAD: That brochure they sent us? They want perfect reputations and a particular kinna build even. She was too topheavy as it was. They give physicals, you know.

MOM: *Wash your hands!*

(Beat)

DAD: O K. O K.

(DAD puts down sandwich. Exits into kitchen as BILLY passes out of it)

BILLY: *(Looking at hands)* Greasy gook. I scrubbed so hard I'm bleeding.

MOM: I'm going shopping. You want anything special?

BILLY: *(Sitting at table)* Yeah. A '56 Chevy.

MOM: Don't complain, ignatz. It's a car, isn't it?

BILLY: A klunky dork on wheels. *(Picks up sandwich)* Pukey! *Liver?*

MOM: Liver*wurst*. And ham. I made two ham.

BILLY: How can you tell? What if I went and bit *into* it?

(MOM, shaking her head, goes to kitchen door.)

MOM: Honey? I'm going shopping. See you later.

DAD: *(From kitchen)* O K, sweetie.

BILLY: *(Mimics)* "O K, sweetie."

MOM: *(Batting him affectionately)* Pipe down.

(Exit MOM, left.)

(Silence, as BILLY carefully bites into a sandwich.)

(Enter DAD.)

DAD: *(Sitting, with a sigh)* Oh my my my my my.

BILLY: *(Indicating sandwich plate)* Liverwurst. I get ham.

DAD: Better not be Spam, that's all. Ever since the Army, I can't eat Spam.

BILLY: Me neither.

DAD: Don't be cute at me. *(Eating)* You should pray you never have to fight. *(Beat)* Army'd whip you into shape. *(Beat)* War. It's a terrible thing.

BILLY: Long's I don't haveta grease cars.

DAD: Cutemouth. *(Puts down sandwich)* Now. After lunch? We gonna go over that engine. I want you to know plugs. Points. Carburetor. Pistons. And how they connect up. Here. *(Takes a pad and clip pencil out of his breast pocket)*

BILLY: Dad? I'm eating here.

DAD: *(Drawing in pad)* O K. Here's the block.

BILLY: The what?

DAD: The block. The basic gut of your car. It cracks and you can throw the whole thing away.

BILLY: Dad?

DAD: Now inside the block. Depending of course on if it's a V-8 or a -6—

BILLY: Did you date girls in Chicago?

(Beat)

DAD: What?

BILLY: When you was a kid.

(DAD stares at BILLY.)

DAD: And the points. Inside the block. Gotta be ignited.

BILLY: Can I get it painted at least? That turdy green and offwhite it's like—

DAD: *(Slamming down pencil)* Who cares! What it looks like? *(Beat)* A thing. On the outside? Is nothin'! It's the inside of a thing that counts. You gotta know. How a thing works. Put your hands in there and. *(Gropes)* Make sure it's workin' right. Some smartass ridin' around don't know the inside of his car? Is prob'ly a careless stupid who stands there! On the side of the freeway. With his fire-engine red busted-down Buick and cryin'! Like a. *(Gropes. Into his son's face)* Like a *woman*!

(Beat)

(BILLY is staring down at plate.)

(DAD eats.)

DAD: Finish your sandwich.

(BILLY *nibbles, looking down.*)

DAD: You got dating on your mind?

BILLY: *(Resentfully)* Why do you think I want the car?

DAD: So. All this I just told you. I should yack at the lamps. *(Beat)* A car ain't for *cruisin'*. *(Beat)* A car? Is for a use.

BILLY: Girls are a use.

DAD: You ain't even got a learner's permit yet. You can't pick up girls anyhow, so stop thinkin' about it.

(They eat.)

(Pause)

DAD: When I was in the Army?

BILLY: Yeah?

DAD: You can catch things.

BILLY: What things?

DAD: Things. You gotta be careful. Little crawly things.

BILLY: *(Eagerly)* Yeah? In the Army?

DAD: Toilet seats. Towels. Sometimes on people's bodies. Girls too.

BILLY: Yeah? Where on girls?

DAD: They're everywhere. You can get 'em off anything. You only got this one body, so keep it clean.

BILLY: Wow. You got cooties off a *girl*?

DAD: Just be careful, that's all! They got medicine it's not a federal case. Forget I said it. *(Beat)* Just be careful.

BILLY: Wow.

(They eat in silence.)

BILLY: So what else?

DAD: What else what?

(DAD puts down his sandwich and starts to draw. BILLY watches him.)

DAD: This. Is your carburetor.

BILLY: Dad? When was the first time you did it? Was it in a car?

(DAD angrily slams down pencil.)

DAD: What are you, a moron?

BILLY: Was it with Mom?

DAD: What?

BILLY: What's the girl feel?

DAD: What do you care?

BILLY: But Dad. We never. Talked about this.

DAD: *O K! (Shrugs)* So now you know.

BILLY: O K.

(DAD resumes drawing, BILLY watching him.)

(DAD shows him drawing.)

DAD: So this. Like I said. It's a carburetor. Which mixes your gas and some air. It sits underneath the air cleaner, O K? *(Draws)* Here's the air cleaner.

BILLY: *(Impish; pointing)* What's that?

DAD: I'll get to that. So the choke plate on the carb lets in the air—

BILLY: Can I see your pencil?

DAD: What?

(BILLY takes pencil; draws.)

DAD: What are you doing?

BILLY: Air. I'm drawing in the air. Little circles. See?

DAD: *(Yanking away pencil)* Gimme the pencil. *(Referring to drawing)* Now in the old days we had manual chokes but now it's automatic. You gotta have like a sixteen-to-one air-to-gas ratio for idling, and then you want like twelve to thirteen parts air to go full throttle.

BILLY: What's that there?

DAD: That's a cam, I'll get to that. Now all this gotta be adjusted or you can't start your car in the morning. So these solenoids—

BILLY: *(Giggling) Solenoids?*

DAD: Yeah?

BILLY: Sounds weird. Like. *(Beat)* Hey, you stupid solenoid.

DAD: Would you pay attention here?

(BILLY grabs pencil from DAD.)

BILLY: *(Drawing)* You should shade in this part. Gives you depth. See?

DAD: *(Angrily; grabbing pencil back) What are you, Walt Disney? (Beat)* I got this car so you could learn about it before you start drivin'. I don't want my kid out there hot roddin' around like a moron with *no respect* for what it is.

BILLY: You can't cherry around in no '54 Chevy.

DAD: *(Repressing his anger)* Now, this air cleaner sits up here and it got a filter. You gotta have clean air in your system or you gonna misfire it could be dangerous on the freeway. So you change that filter when it gets dirty. Remember that, in the fuel system of your car, cleanliness is next to godliness.

BILLY: Sure.

DAD: And a two-barrel carb is a damn expensive thing so you gotta keep all your adjustments right. You got the idle circuit, the acceleration circuit—

BILLY: Is Sharon gonna drive the car?

(Beat)

DAD: What?

BILLY: When she gets back. You gonna tell her all this?

DAD: She's a *girl*! She can drive it, sure. But basically it's gonna be your responsibility. You keep it runnin' good and it won't break down on her. A girl out there in a broke-down car? Is like helpless. You want your sister out there all helpless?

(Beat)

BILLY: No.

DAD: So pay attention. *(Points at drawing)* So what's this?

BILLY: A solenoid?

DAD: *(Shaking head)* This! is a solenoid. Here. Is the choke plate.

BILLY: The way you draw I can't tell. There's no contrast or nothin'. *(Takes pencil)* See, if you just put some shadow here then—

DAD: *You want the back of my hand?*

(BILLY drops pencil.)

(DAD pours himself a shot, drinks it.)

(Silence)

DAD: *(Not looking at BILLY)* When I was a kid I woulda died to have a car. I usta hang around garages just to look inside 'em.

(Silence)

BILLY: Dad?

DAD: Finish your sandwich.

BILLY: Remember that time you gave me a shot of whiskey and I threw up?

DAD: *(Smiles)* Yeah. *(Sententious)* Drinkin's like drivin'. Kids shouldn't do it. So you learned somethin' that time. *(Points at drawing)* I wish you'd learn somethin' here.

(Beat)

BILLY: Remember when you usta walk around naked in front of us? And told Sharon to look at you?

(DAD stares at BILLY.)

DAD: You're a moron.

BILLY: But you did.

DAD: So? It's O K when kids are little. Kids can take a gander it's a natural thing to know.

BILLY: But Mom didn't.

DAD: For chrissakes! You want your mother walkin' around here like a naked floozy?

BILLY: No.

DAD: Why'd you bring that up?

BILLY: What up?

DAD: That about me. Why?

BILLY: I dunno.

DAD: What's goin' on in your head? *(Rises from chair)* I'm startin' to think you're kinna funny like.

(DAD crosses to plate glass. Looks out at yard. Lights a cigarette)

(BILLY looks down at plate.)

DAD: *(Over his shoulder)* And I don't mean ha-ha. *(Beat; looking out)* It was O K. *(Over shoulder)* You're the funny one. *(He throws open plate glass door, leans against frame, looking out.)*

(Beat)

BILLY: Do you miss her? Dad?

DAD: Who?

BILLY: Sharon. I think about her. A whole lot.

(Beat)

DAD: Me too.

(Silence)

(BILLY picks up drawing. DAD continues looking out.)

BILLY: Dad?

(No response)

BILLY: O K. So. This is the air cleaner. And this is the carburetor. It mixes up the air and gas and then what?

(No response)

BILLY: Dad?

DAD: *(Dragging on cigarette; looking out)* It goes down the intake manifold to the combustion chamber.

BILLY: And then what?

DAD: You got spark plugs pokin' in there.

BILLY: In the chamber? Where the gas goes?

(DAD nods, looking out.)

BILLY: And what happens?

(Beat)

DAD: It explodes.

(Lights dim to black.)

(Sound track: the opening bars of "Love Is Strange" by Mickey & Sylvia)

(Lights up. Music continues into:)

Scene Five

(Evening, six months later. Drapes are drawn.)

(BILLY is sitting at table, a book open before him.)

(Enter SHARON in outsized man's shirt and skintight jeans. She is heavily made up. She has two empty beer bottles in her hand.)

(BILLY watches her cross to kitchen. She doesn't look at him.)

(Music fades. As she passes:)

SHARON: So go out.

(SHARON exits into kitchen.)

(BILLY sits, staring at book.)

(Reenter SHARON, with two full beer bottles. Not looking at her brother, she crosses left. As she does so:)

SHARON: You can't get a date? Just this once?

(Exit SHARON into front room, left.)

(BILLY continues reading, desultorily.)

(Reenter SHARON, *empty-handed. She crosses to kitchen, not looking at* BILLY. *To him:)*

SHARON: Go see a movie.

(Exit SHARON *into kitchen.)*

*(*BILLY *grips the corners of his book.)*

(Reenter SHARON, *with bag of potato chips.)*

SHARON: Or something.

(She crosses left.)

BILLY: *(Pointing offstage, left)* He gonna stay all night?

SHARON: *(Pausing to look at* BILLY*)* None. Of your business.

BILLY: He gonna play loud music all night?

SHARON: So go in your room at least.

BILLY: They come back tomorrow. Dad'll kill you all this beer and.

(Pause)

SHARON: Billy. Don't be creepoid.

BILLY: What if they come back early?

SHARON: Not from Tahoe. It'll be— *(Gesturing into front room)* All. Cleaned. Up.

BILLY: They'll notice. *(Gesturing off)* He's a slob.

SHARON: From twenty thousand fathoms.

BILLY: Yeah.

SHARON: That's you. The one from twenty thousand fathoms.

(Exit SHARON, *left.)*

*(*BILLY *slams book shut, rises, exits into kitchen.)*

*(*BILLY *reenters with a carrot. Sits, gnaws)*

(Enter SHARON.*)*

SHARON: *(Hands on hips)* So?

BILLY: *(Munching)* Huh?

SHARON: So go out. Bobby doesn't like it you're hanging around.

BILLY: He doesn't.

SHARON: No.

*(*BILLY *munches away.)*

SHARON: Not one girl. You can't get. One girl.

(BILLY *same*)

SHARON: Or friends even. Not one friend.

(BILLY *same*)

SHARON: I thought. You know what I thought? (*Beat*) You woulda changed while I was back east. (*Beat*) But you're just like before. (*Beat*) Grow up, Billy. And go out somewhere.

(*Offstage male voice calls: "Sherry!"*)

BILLY: (*Mimics*) "Sherry."

SHARON: (*Exiting*) Coming, Bobby!

(BILLY *gnaws on carrot.*)

(*Reenter* SHARON, *crossing into kitchen.*)

(*She reenters with fresh bottle of beer.*)

BILLY: Beer breath all night.

SHARON: Shut up and go to a movie.

BILLY: I ain't got the money.

SHARON: You always got money.

BILLY: Ain't.

SHARON: (*Pointing at him with bottle*) I borrowed. (*Moves closer*) I borrowed five dollars from you and you. Charged me. Interest.

BILLY: So?

SHARON: So don't tell me you don't have it.

BILLY: (*Gesturing off*) Ask beer belly.

(*Beat*)

SHARON: You. Fucker.

(*Exit* SHARON, *left.*)

(BILLY *stops gnawing, stares at table.*)

(*Reenter* SHARON; BILLY *abruptly starts munching.*)

SHARON: He's getting mad. (*Beat*) Billy? He'll cream you.

BILLY: I'm so scared. Look at me.

SHARON: (*Placating*) Just for a couple of hours. That's all. Please, Billy.

BILLY: What you gonna do in there? I don't bother you.

SHARON: Don't be stupoid.

BILLY: A pack of Winston.

(Muttering, she exits left.)

(BILLY makes a show of feeling his muscle.)

(SHARON reenters with a pack of cigarettes. Throws it on table.)

BILLY: Thanks. I needed a cigarette.

(He lights up, luxuriously puffs.)

SHARON: You smoke like a dork. *(Beat)* So? Go somewhere.

BILLY: *(Sitting back)* Thanks for the cigarettes.

(She lunges for pack, he grabs it, they struggle.)

(Offstage male voice calls, "Hey Sherry. What's up?")

(She gives up struggle.)

SHARON: *(Calling off)* It's O K. *(To BILLY)* Liar. Fucker.

BILLY: Dork, huh?

SHARON: The way you smoke. The way you walk.

BILLY: I should smoke like your boyfriend maybe. *(Hunches over, cups hand around cigarette. To her, in gruff voice)* Gimme a beer. *(Huge contempt)* "Sherry."

SHARON: You're not funny anymore. You never were.

BILLY: *(Sprawling in chair)* Hey, baby. *(Fake belch)* I wanna beer. Come on, chick. Gimme a beer. *(Beat; normal voice)* Then I drink it it goes all down my chin and I make you kiss my slimey mouth. *(Resuming normal position in chair)* I'd rather be a dork.

SHARON: That's good. Because you are.

BILLY: Yeah?

SHARON: Yeah.

BILLY: Maybe I should sit around and fart like your boyfriend.

SHARON: He doesn't fart.

BILLY: Then you'd think I was Mr Tough Guy.

SHARON: Tough. You. With your '54 Chevy.

BILLY: *(Bridling)* Shut up.

SHARON: Scag wagon. Queermobile.

BILLY: *(Angry now)* Queer, huh?

SHARON: They say so.

BILLY: Queer, huh?

SHARON: If the shoe fits.

BILLY: *Then how come—?*

(They stare at each other.)

(SHARON angrily exits, left.)

(BILLY sits, staring after her.)

(BILLY rises, exits into kitchen.)

(Reenter BILLY with beer. He sits, chugalugs it.)

(Reenter SHARON, beer in hand. She poses with bottle, biker style, staring at her brother)

SHARON: Bobby wants to talk to you.

BILLY: So?

SHARON: Hey. Where'd you get that beer?

BILLY: Kitchen.

SHARON: That's Bobby's beer.

BILLY: Gee.

SHARON: Frip.

BILLY: Who's a frip? He wants to talk to me? He can get off his ass and come in here.

SHARON: Such a tough—

BILLY: Give me no orders.

SHARON: Bunny.

BILLY: I wanna reefer.

(Beat)

SHARON: *(Contemptuously)* You. A reefer.

BILLY: *(Gesturing at front room)* He's the big man at Harvey's Drive-In, he got reefer.

SHARON: So?

BILLY: So tell him.

(Beat)

SHARON: If I get you a reefer. Will you go out somewhere?

BILLY: Sure, chickie.

(SHARON exits into front room. BILLY quickly leans forward, listening.)

(Offstage male voice: "A what?")

(BILLY snickers and buries his head in book again.)

(SHARON *reenters;* BILLY *lowers book below eyes.*)

SHARON: *(Holding up J)* This. Is so. Fine. *(Lowers it to his face)* What a waste.

BILLY: *(Staring at J)* Can you die from it?

(Beat, as SHARON *reacts disdainfully)*

BILLY: I mean, if you smoke too much?

(SHARON stares in contempt; drops J on table. He puts down book, picks up J.)

BILLY: This. Is it.

SHARON: Light it.

BILLY: *(Examining J)* What end?

SHARON: God.

(She takes J.)

SHARON: *(Gesturing)* This end. Or this end. With a match.

(She starts to light it; He takes J and matches.)

BILLY: You a *real* low-rider? A real low-rider mama?

SHARON: Kissie. Light it. *(Watches as he fumbles with J and matches)* Kissie.

BILLY: *(Puffing)* We'll do like at Harvey's. You be like. My low-rider mama. *(Coughs; blows smoke about)* My chiquita.

(She grabs J.)

SHARON: Don't waste it. Like this.

(She inhales hissingly, holds it, exhales, hands back J.)

BILLY: I get you. *(He inhales, holds it. Gasping:)* How long. I gotta. Hold it?

SHARON: *(Sitting; exasperated)* Fudd.

BILLY: *(Same)* How long?

(She sits, waiting.)

(BILLY exhales coughingly. Beat)

BILLY: I don't feel nothin.

SHARON: Farmer. Take some more.

(Again he inhales, hissingly.)

SHARON: You're gonna get sick.

(Again he exhales, coughing.)

(She giggles.)

BILLY: *(Sprawling in chair; indicating J)* This ain't so tough.

SHARON: Goody gumdrops. With a reefer.

BILLY: I'm as bad as anybody.

SHARON: Yeah? *(She takes J, inhales, hands it back.)* So why don't you go out. To like Harvey's? And prove it.

BILLY: Maybe I will.

SHARON: *(Contemptuously)* In your '54 Chevy.

BILLY: *(Into her face)* Maybe I'll pick up a slut!

(Beat)

(Angrily, she plucks J from his fingers. Rises, stands over him, J in her mouth, hand on her hip, biker-style, defiant and provocative.)

SHARON: Maybe she'll laugh at you.

(He also stands, taking J from her lips.)

BILLY: Maybe she won't.

(They are nose to nose.)

SHARON: She'd laugh at your dorkie clothes.

BILLY: *(Mimics Bobby)* Come on, chick. Gimme some.

SHARON: At your dorkie glasses.

BILLY: Gimme gimme.

SHARON: At your dorkie car.

BILLY: Shut up!

SHARON: At your creepy walk and your fairy talk and your—

BILLY: *Gimme!*

(Violently, he embraces his sister, crushing his mouth against hers. She struggles.)

SHARON: Stop it!

(Offstage male voice: "Sherry?")

(SHARON and BILLY break; she crosses in direction of front room.)

SHARON: *(Angrily calling off)* Just a minute!

(She slowly crosses back to BILLY.)

(SHARON spits in BILLY's face.)

(BILLY closes his eyes; otherwise does not react.)

(Offstage male voice: "Sherry! What the hell?")

SHARON: *(Still staring at her brother)* Coming, Bobby. *(Beat)* Want another beer? Bobby? *(Beat)* Whatever you want, Bobby. Just ask.

(BILLY *discards J on table, marches out of room.*)

SHARON: *(To herself; triumphant)* Whatever. You. Want.

(Blackout)

(Sound track: the opening bars of "Daddy's Home" by Shep & the Limelights)

(Music fades. Lights up on:)

Scene Six

(Dinnertime, three months later. Drapes open. DAD and MOM sit glumly at table, on which is a whiskey bottle, glasses, and a bowl of corn chips, dry and crackling, from which they periodically eat.)

(Silence. Then:)

DAD: Christ almighty god. *(He drinks)*

MOM: I know.

DAD: *(Louder)* Christ Jesus.

MOM: Well, we raised her. *(She drinks, makes a face)*

DAD: Don't gimme that. That crap we raised her.

MOM: I know.

(Beat)

DAD: This time. The guy marries her.

MOM: I suppose.

DAD: She out with him?

MOM: They went to Harvey's.

DAD: *(Huge contempt)* Harvey's.

MOM: Doesn't matter now. Where she goes.

DAD: What's he do?

MOM: Drop out. Seven-eleven.

DAD: You mean like that liquor store?

MOM: *(Drinking, with a shrug)* Beer and wine. Says he guesses.
He'll marry her.

DAD: Jesus H Christ. Seven-eleven. She was going to *airline* school!

MOM: Billy can go to college.

DAD: Some stumblebum offa Seven-eleven. Jesus H Almighty God.
She won't even graduate high school.

MOM: Oh well. I guess they'd let her. If she weren't—

DAD: *(Bitterly; refilling glass)* Knocked up again.

MOM: Anyway. I guess he'll marry her. Says he will. Strangest thing.

DAD: What's so strange a stumblebum?

MOM: He reminds me of guys during. The war. Girls too. Nobody cared. Just. Get married.

DAD: What are you? We cared. We knew what we were doing.

MOM: Honey. We got married. Fast.

DAD: So? It was different then. Anyways. A guy coulda died. And we loved each other. That's the difference. She can't love that.

MOM: She doesn't. She told me so.

(Beat)

DAD: You mean. She's not gonna go through with it?

MOM: No. She knows she's got to this time.

DAD: *(Relieved)* My little girl. To a cashier. At a liquor-eleven. We didn't raise her for this.

MOM: We raised her.

DAD: Would you cut out this we raised her crap? Look at me. My stepdad in Chicago. Threw me out I was fourteen years old. Middle the Depression. Did I go out and mess around? At Harvey's?

MOM: It's harder for a girl.

DAD: I never had a chance go to airline college. *(Bangs table) She spits on us!*

(Beat; he drinks.)

MOM: Billy can go to college.

DAD: *(Frowning as he drinks)* Billy.

MOM: He's O K.

DAD: Something. I dunno. Wrong there.

MOM: Honey? He's all right.

DAD: Sharon was my little girl. Remember I usta drive with her in my lap? She was just a button but she'd put her little hands on the wheel and play like she was drivin'. We'd go faster and faster and faster and faster. She couldn't get enough and she loved it. *Laugh?* Boy, could she laugh. *(Drinks)* It was right after they put in the Santa Ana. Jesus.

MOM: Billy's never been in trouble.

DAD: You grew up that old bastard out in Riverside that apricot farm? Wouldn't even let you go to a dance. You whoored around? No. Never. *(Drinks) Jesus.*

MOM: *(Drinking also)* There's nothing wrong with Billy.

DAD: I dunno.

MOM: He's O K.

DAD: Somethin'. Funny.

MOM: Don't make a federal case. *(Rising)* You want supper? I could make. A meat loaf.

DAD: *(Shakes head; pouring)* Drink up.

(She sits. They drink.)

DAD: What makes her do these things? Sweetie? What?

MOM: It's like they don't care.

DAD: *(Exploding) What you mean they don't care! (Mimics wildly)* "They don't care!" "They don't care!" *(Beat)* Now. I asked you a question.

MOM: *(Drinking)* I don't know.

DAD: Why don't you know?

MOM: Stop it.

DAD: I. Asked you. A question.

MOM: She did it. To hurt. *(Beat; not looking at* DAD*)* Us.

DAD: *Crap! (Beat)* She was my little girl.

MOM: Honey. She hasn't been your little girl. In a long time.

DAD: I was in Germany. So goddamned wet and with filth. I get your letter and I can't stop tellin' the guys. I said I wanted a boy. Gotta have a boy.

MOM: You were tickled pink when you saw her.

DAD: Oh, man. She was so cute. I wanted. To gobble her up, *(Beat; quickly)* What's wrong with that?

MOM: I didn't say it was—

DAD: I loved her! Right down here in my guts I loved her. *(Bitterly)* Hurt us. *(Beat)* Crap. It was when she got tits.

MOM: *(Shaking her head)* Oh, honey.

DAD: Twelve was awful young for tits that big.

MOM: It wasn't that.

DAD: It was that.

MOM: No.

DAD: It makes sense! *(Mimics again)* "They don't care!" "Hurt us!"
That makes. No. Sense. If you're gonna talk to me. Make. Sense. *(Beat)*
You hear me?

MOM: *(Rising)* I better get supper.

DAD: *Sit down! (Beat)* And talk to me.

(She sits.)

DAD: She just go outa here and said. You tell Dad? And left with this
stumblebum for. Harvey's?

MOM: I guess so.

DAD: That place. Is like a Marineland of Mexican. Or white grease oughta be
Mexican. Drive around and around the parking lot what kinna fun is that?
(Beat) We went to the Hollywood Palladium.

MOM: *(Drinking)* I cried.

DAD: You what?

MOM: When Glen Miller got killed. I cried.

DAD: Sure. The big bands. We was lucky to find somebody hadda car.
We didn't drive around and around. *(Beat)* And around and around. *(Beat)*
And around and around and around. *(He bangs table.)*

MOM: Honey. I told her she could go. Said *I'd* tell you. Don't worry, I said.
Just go.

DAD: You told her that.

MOM: And I gave Billy some money for gas. He won't go to Harvey's.
I just wanted us. To be alone here.

DAD: Alone here.

MOM: It's best. *(Beat)* Billy'll go. To Hollywood.

DAD: *(Contemptuous)* Hollywood.

MOM: The bookstores.

DAD: *(Drinking)* Hollywood is not. What it was. We hadda job out to
Westwood just this twelve-inch it was a piece of cake. So anyways.
We seen this pansy on Hollywood Boulevard. Walkin' a *poodle.*

MOM: Honey. He goes to the bookstores.

DAD: Faggots go to bookstores! Who you think buys all those books?

(Beat; they are distinctly drunk.)

MOM: It's wrong. What we're doing. *(Hands to her face)* She shouldn't.
Marry him.

DAD: Nobody give me a car. I was in the eighth grade my stepdad says. Get out. With this *crowbar* in his hand. Just like that. Puts me on the street with a crowbar.

MOM: *(Looking up; suddenly angry)* Your mother.

DAD: Middle the Depression.

MOM: *(Same)* Your mother. How could she just stand by? Let that old. Son of a.

(Overlapping:)

DAD: Ended up on the goddamn federal works.

MOM: *(Making fists)* She was so self-righteous about Sharon. So pure. So *religious*.

DAD: Nobody gave me a goddamn. Four in the morning.

MOM: And she just.

DAD: I'd get up. Four in the morning. Winter and summer.

MOM: She didn't love you. *(Beat)*

DAD: Who didn't?

MOM: Your mother.

DAD: My mother?

MOM: All that about her sacrifices. And she stood there while that son of a gun put you on the street. To starve.

DAD: She couldn't help it.

MOM: Oh, no. Couldn't help it.

(Overlapping:)

DAD: It's still dark at four in the morning.

MOM: Just stood there. Watching. If *you* tried that.

DAD: Winter mornings back east? You can't see your hand it's so dark.

MOM: If you tried that with Billy.

DAD: And they turn into whoors. Right in your face.

MOM: I'd stop you. I swear it.

DAD: Weekends those kids sleep 'til noon!

MOM: I'd stop you or I'd. Go with him.

DAD: Sashayin' down Hollywood Boulevard.

MOM: It's got. To stop.

DAD: Or some taco wagon at Harvey's—well, this time she *marries* the taco wagon!

MOM: *(Exploding)* It's got to stop!

(Silence)

(She sits, head in hands. DAD looks away. Drinks)

DAD: You better get supper.

MOM: *(Head still in hands)* Scrambled eggs. I could scramble some eggs.

DAD: Sure.

MOM: *(Dropping hands)* With onions.

(Beat)

DAD: Sweetie. I'm tired.

MOM: Hard. *(Beat; looking at him)* Day?

DAD: La Puente. Hell and gone.

MOM: *(Rising)* Honey?

DAD: Yeah?

MOM: You always. Put the food on the table. *(Touches his shoulder tenderly; a wan smile)* And you never ran around on me.

(He covers her hand with his.)

(They stare at table.)

(Lights dim to black.)

(Sound track: the opening bars of "Come On, Let's Go" by Richie Valens)

(Lights up. Music continues into:)

Scene Seven

(Morning, two weeks later. The drapes are opened, and the brilliant California sunshine pours in through the plate glass, gilding the room. A small wedding cake and plastic flower arrangement on the table. A plate of finger sandwiches and napkins.)

(BILLY is standing and looking out onto patio, snapping his fingers to the music. He is dressed in flecked sports jacket and slacks.)

(SHARON, seated at table, is dressed in cream-colored tailored suit and tiara, looking into a compact and fussing with her hair and makeup.)

(Music out. BILLY moves into room, sits at table.)

BILLY: *(Taking out cigarette)* Hey, chickie. You look good.

SHARON: *(Into compact)* I know.

BILLY: *Real* good.

SHARON: Thanks.

BILLY: I mean. Like a model.

(She notices he is lighting up.)

SHARON: Better not, Billy. Mom and Dad only went out for liquor. They won't like it they catch you smoking.

(BILLY shrugs, lights up. Exhales)

BILLY: So when we gotta be there?

SHARON: By noon.

BILLY: Why there? In that church? We ain't religious.

SHARON: Bobby's parents.

BILLY: They're weird.

SHARON: You can put up with them this once. It's just us. And them. *(Snapping compact shut; ironically:)* It's a quiet affair.

BILLY: Their house is weird. Okieville.

SHARON: Daddy likes them O K.

BILLY: No, he don't. And Mom don't either. Okies.

SHARON: So? Mom's people were Tennessee.

BILLY: But Mom was *born* in California. She's first generation.

SHARON: Big deal.

BILLY: Mom says. Bobby's folks are white trash. *(Laughs)* And Dad says yeah but anyways they're white.

SHARON: *(Also laughing; in spite of herself)* He's. Something. He really thought. I'd marry a Negro.

BILLY: All that Johnny Otis on T V. *(Snapping fingers; sings:)* "De bop bama looma, de bop bam boom!"

SHARON: Daddy's such a. *(Stops laughing)* Jerk.

BILLY: Yeah. *(Beat)* He thinks I'm queer.

(SHARON looks away.)

SHARON: I just wanna. Get this over with.

BILLY: So you guys gonna live here? Or in Bell Gardens?

SHARON: With Bobby's folks? No way.

BILLY: God. That refrigerator torn apart on the front lawn? God, That car torn apart in the driveway? God. They just cut the grass around the spare parts.

SHARON: *When* they cut the grass. No. Way.

BILLY: So here?

SHARON: Daddy's giving us. Some money for an apartment. In Norwalk.

BILLY: Norwalk's Mexican!

SHARON: Only until. The baby comes. Then I guess. Someplace.

BILLY: The baby.

SHARON: *(Laughing)* You're not supposed to know.

BILLY: I can figure it out.

SHARON: I dunno. So can everybody else. *(Looks at table)* This is stupid.

BILLY: Even the cake is sad.

(Beat)

SHARON: *(Checking watch)* Where are they?

BILLY: Prob'ly bought some liquor then stopped off for a drink. They been drinkin' like fishoids.

SHARON: Guess what?

BILLY: What?

SHARON: Dad said. I didn't have to go through with it.

BILLY: When?

SHARON: The other night. Can you believe it?

BILLY: He didn't mean it.

SHARON: I know. But wasn't that—?

BILLY: Oh sure. And what? Send you back east to Grandma's? Do it all over again?

SHARON: Shut up! *(Beat)* That. Didn't happen.

BILLY: Crapola.

(Beat. BILLY begins tasting frosting of cake with his fingertip.)

SHARON: Stop that.

(He continues.)

SHARON: Billy!

BILLY: *(Tasting)* It's gooey.

SHARON: Leave it. Alone.

BILLY: It's funny. Just sitting there. All squatty. And these dippy little sandwiches!

SHARON: They're supposed to be *elegant*.

BILLY: *(Shaking head over food)* Mom sure hates to cook.

SHARON: *(Giggling)* Yeah. Look at that cake.

BILLY: She shoulda put onions in it.

SHARON: A liver wedding cake!

(They bust up giggling.)

BILLY: Hey. Look at me. *(Makes a heavy moronic face)*

SHARON: What are you doing?

BILLY: I'm Bobby. *(Points at sandwiches; holds one up)* And this. Is you. Watch. *(Shoves it into his mouth. Eats grossly as his sister stares)*

SHARON: *Stop it!*

(She rises, looking away. BILLY ceases moronic eating, wipes mouth.)

SHARON: God, everybody's right. You're such a—

BILLY: *(Cutting her off)* Know what I think?

SHARON: Who cares?

BILLY: I think we shoulda gone away. To like. Seal Beach. I coulda learned to surf. We coulda raised it.

SHARON: Are you. Crazy?

BILLY: Or Hollywood. They never woulda found us in Hollywood.

(SHARON begins laughing; sits; between giggles:)

SHARON: Kids at school. Think you're. But you're not. Know what you are? You're a *loon*!

BILLY: Maybe I am. Queer.

(She stops laughing.)

BILLY: Everybody says so. So maybe I am.

SHARON: It's just the way you. Act.

BILLY: But if everybody says it. Maybe I should be it. Dad don't say it. But he thinks it.

SHARON: That's not. True.

BILLY: But if everybody wants me to be queer, then maybe I should be! I mean. *(Shakes head)* God.

SHARON: *(Softly)* Don't. Let them.

BILLY: Don't let them what?

SHARON: Make you queer.

BILLY: Oh? Like they're making you. *(Points at cake)* Do this?

SHARON: Be quiet.

BILLY: *(Eagerly)* We could run away. Right now. We should raise this one like we shoulda raised the other one!

SHARON: *(Rising from chair) Shut up! (Beat; fidgeting)* This is Bobby's baby I'm gonna be Bobby's wife; you're crazy.

BILLY: The other one was mine!

SHARON: *Forget that!* That didn't. Happen. That should never—

BILLY: Dennis. It wasn't no Dennis.

SHARON: *(Jabbing finger at him)* Don't you say this to Bobby. Don't you. *Ever.* Mention this to. *Anybody.*

BILLY: Dennis was a hot air. Just like Bobby.

SHARON: What did I just say?

BILLY: *(Stubbornly)* The other one was mine.

SHARON: It was. Not.

BILLY: You said so!

SHARON: Because I wanted— *(Beat; sadly)* To hurt you. *(She fidgets with flower arrangements.)*

BILLY: Oh. Thanks a lot.

SHARON: *(Mimics)* "Thanks a lot." Shit. *(Beat)* I had to. Take it all. You would just sit here and nothing—

BILLY: Bull.

SHARON: Ever happened to you.

BILLY: Yeah? So what about that time he makes me go into Little League?

SHARON: *It's not the same! (Beat; disdainfully:)* Little League. God.

BILLY: Dad said he was gonna Scotch Tape my mitt to my hand.

SHARON: *(Laughing)* You sure looked funnoid in that uniform.

BILLY: Not as funny as Dad. When he usta walk around naked in front of us?

SHARON: *(Uneasily; moving to plate glass)* Billy.

BILLY: Remember? Always said. Take a gander. *(Rises, imitates fowl)* "Take a gander! Take a gander!" *(Laughing)* What's that, like a goose?

(SHARON *laughs, remembering.*)

SHARON: That pot belly!

BILLY: Those knobby knees!

SHARON: God!

BILLY: Come on, let's do the Gander Stomp!

SHARON: Do the Stewardess Stomp!

(*Using arms and elbows as wings, they stomp about, laughing.*)

(*Suddenly,* BILLY *grabs* SHARON.)

BILLY: Sharon, it wasn't no Dennis!

(*She breaks away from him.*)

SHARON: It was so!

(*She returns to plate glass, looks out. He sits.*)

(*Beat*)

BILLY: (*Disdainfully*) Dennis.

(SHARON *is silent, indifferent, looking out at backyard.*)

BILLY: Said he used a rubber.

(SHARON *freezes.*)

BILLY: Dennis told it all over school how he used one.

SHARON: (*Not looking at him*) He. What?

BILLY: Said he took *precaution*. Such a big man. I knew he was full of it.

(*Beat, as* SHARON *continues staring out*)

SHARON: He *was*. Full of it. (*Turns, looks at* BILLY) You all are.

BILLY: It was mine!

SHARON: *So! Fucking! What?* (*Beat. She sits.*) You're supposed to be. Happy. On your wedding day. But I feel. Like. I have to catch a bus.

BILLY: Like the first day of the school year. All queasy.

SHARON: Uh-huh. Like it's gonna be a long time.

BILLY: Until summer.

SHARON: Yeah.

(*They stare at cake.*)

BILLY: I'm a queer and you're a slut. So we should. Go away.

SHARON: (*Rising*) Go to hell.

BILLY: It was my baby. And you let them—

SHARON: *Let* them?

BILLY: Give it away.

SHARON: Oh. Right. I shoulda given it to you. Oh. I see. And you coulda. Dressed it up. In little frillies? And played with it.

BILLY: Shut up.

SHARON: Billy. You had nothing to do with that. Guys don't. You're just. Things.

BILLY: *I* was?

SHARON: *(Offhand; cynical)* Sure. Guys are just things. Licking. And biting. Then they marry you and you live in Norwalk.

BILLY: I. Was this *thing* to you?

SHARON: *(Same)* Sure. I didn't feel anything. I never feel anything. *(Beat)*

(BILLY slowly rises and picks a plastic flower out of arrangement.)

BILLY: A thing. Like this?

(He tosses flower at her; no reaction)

BILLY: A rubbery. *(Picks another)* Fake. *(Throws flower violently into her face)* Thing!

(SHARON turns away, rubbing her cheek. BILLY sits, stares at floor.)

SHARON: Billy. I'm really sorry. About all. That. So just forget it, O K?

BILLY: *(Mimics)* "Just forget it, O K?"

SHARON: *(Looks at watch)* They did stop for a drink. *(Looking at table)* We better put the flowers back. *(Laughing)* For the *reception. (She picks up plastic flowers from floor, then all at once twirls, girlishly, irrepressibly, then replaces flowers. Fussing:)* You'll get married someday.

BILLY: Queers don't get married.

SHARON: Oh, Billy. *(She sits down again, crosses her hands in her lap, demurely:)* You will. Someday.

(BILLY makes a flatulent noise with his lips.)

SHARON: *(Smiling)* You're just a kid.

BILLY: Oh, hey. *(Rises)* Here we got. *(Gesturing)* The old married lady.

SHARON: *(Self-deprecating)* I know.

BILLY: God. You're two years older than me. This is not. A long time.

SHARON: *(Same)* I know.

BILLY: So don't gimme that. Mature crapoid.

SHARON: It changes you. That's all.

BILLY: *I'm* still the same.

SHARON: I meant. Marriage.

BILLY: Oh. You mean. *(Circles table, pointing at cake)* This does? *(Beat)* This sad. Ugly. *(He sinks his hand into cake.)* Thing?

(SHARON stares.)

(Silence)

(She looks away.)

SHARON: Oh well.

(BILLY withdraws hand, looks at it.)

BILLY: *(Extending hand towards her)* Want some?

SHARON: Daddy'll. Kill you.

BILLY: *(Same)* Want some? *(Beat)* Go ahead. *(He thrusts his begooed hand close to her averted face.)* Lick it off my fingers. *(Beat, as slowly she looks at his hand)* Go ahead. *(Thrusts hand)* Lick it!

(Pause)

(SHARON calmly looks from his hand to his face.)

SHARON: You can't.

BILLY: Can't what?

SHARON: *(Shrugging)* Do that. *(Looking away)* I don't live here anymore.

(Slowly BILLY withdraws hand. He seems confused as he looks about at random.)

(Finally, he flicks goo from his hand back into cake.)

BILLY: God. I messed it. Bad.

SHARON: I'll say it was me. That I'm just. I dunno. Nervous.

BILLY: Will you? Sharon?

SHARON: *(Nodding)* Something.

(Meekly, he takes napkin, wipes his hand, sits down again.)

(Silence)

(They stare at floor.)

(All at once SHARON impishly begins humming, then singing, the opening bars to the song "Speedo".)

SHARON: "Well now they often call me Speedo—"

(She looks at BILLY.)

BILLY: *(Picking it up)* "But my real name is—" *(He taps shoe in time. Chiming:)*

SHARON & BILLY: *(In unison)* "Mister Earl."

(They laugh and repeat refrain, SHARON snapping her fingers. BILLY trails off as SHARON continues singing.)

BILLY: *(Under her singing)* Sharon?

(She continues singing.)

BILLY: Was it. A boy?

(She abruptly falls silent.)

BILLY: Or a girl?

SHARON: *(Shrugging)* A boy, I think.

(Beat)

BILLY: Was he. O K?

SHARON: I dunno.

BILLY: You don't. Know?

SHARON: I didn't see him.

BILLY: Didn't even. See him?

SHARON: He wasn't very strong, I think.

BILLY: He wasn't—

(Beat)

SHARON: *(Dropping eyes)* Very strong.

(Sound track: "Speedo" by the Cadillacs)

(Lights dim.)

CURTAIN

BROADWAY PLAY PUBLISHING INC

LONG ONE ACTS
(WRITTEN WITHOUT AN INTERMISSION)

BAL
(IN PLAYS BY RICHARD NELSON
EARLY PLAYS VOLUME TWO)

BEIRUT
(IN PLAYS BY ALAN BOWNE)

BETWEEN EAST AND WEST

THE BEST OF STRANGERS
(IN FACING FORWARD)

FLOOR ABOVE THE ROOF

FLOOR SHOW: DOÑA SOL AND HER TRAINED DOG
(IN PLAYS BY EDWIN SÁNCHEZ)

HAITI (A DREAM)
(IN FACING FORWARD)

HARM'S WAY

THE HELIOTROPE BOUQUET BY SCOTT JOPLIN & LOUIS
CHAUVIN

HOLY DAYS

HOUSE OF SHADOWS
(IN PLAYS BY STEVE CARTER)

ICARUS

BROADWAY PLAY PUBLISHING INC

LONG ONE ACTS (CONT'D)
(WRITTEN WITHOUT AN INTERMISSION)

IS HE STILL DEAD?
(IN PLAYS BY DONALD FREED)

JITTERBUGGING: SCENES OF SEX IN A NEW SOCIETY
(IN PLAYS BY RICHARD NELSON
EARLY PLAYS VOLUME THREE)

JUNGLE COUP
(IN PLAYS BY RICHARD NELSON
EARLY PLAYS VOLUME ONE)

THE NIP AND THE BITE
(IN FACING FORWARD)

THE RETURN OF PINOCCHIO
(IN PLAYS BY RICHARD NELSON
EARLY PLAYS VOLUME TWO)

SEVENTY SCENES OF HALLOWEEN

SHARON AND BILLY
(IN PLAYS BY ALAN BOWNE)

TRAFFICKING IN BROKEN HEARTS
(IN PLAYS BY EDWIN SÁNCHEZ)

UNFINISHED WOMEN CRY IN A NO MAN'S LAND WHILE A
BIRD DIES IN A GILDED CAGE
(IN PLAYS BY AISHAH RAHMAN)

THE VIENNA NOTES
(IN PLAYS BY RICHARD NELSON
EARLY PLAYS VOLUME TWO)

BROADWAY PLAY PUBLISHING INC

THREE CHARACTER PLAYS

BATTERY

BEIRUT
(IN PLAYS BY ALAN BOWNE)

THE BIBLE: THE COMPLETE WORD OF GOD (ABRIDGED)

THE COMPLETE HISTORY OF AMERICA (ABRIDGED)

A DARING BRIDE
(IN PLAYS BY ALLAN HAVIS, VOLUME TWO)

FROM THE JOURNAL OF HAZARD MCCAULEY

JUNGLE COUP
(IN PLAYS BY RICHARD NELSON, EARLY PLAYS VOLUME ONE)

LIPS

MINK SONATA
(IN PLAYS BY ALLAN HAVIS)

PICK UP AX

SUDDEN DEVOTION
(IN PLAYS BY STUART SPENCER)

THREE FRONT
(IN PLAYS BY ROCHELLE OWENS)

TRAFFICKING IN BROKEN HEARTS
(IN PLAYS BY EDWIN SÁNCHEZ)

2 1/2 JEWS